THE FREEDOM OF MAN

THE FREEDOM OF MAN

An Inquiry Into Some Roots
of the Tension Between Freedom
and Authority in Our Society

by T. PAUL VERGHESE

THE WESTMINSTER PRESS
Philadelphia

PUBLISHED BY THE WESTMINSTER PRESS®
PHILADELPHIA, PENNSYLVANIA

PRINTED IN THE UNITED STATES OF AMERICA

Contents

Foreword

I am grateful to the three theological seminaries of the Lutheran Church in America. They gave me a sounding board for some of these ideas, in the form of an invitation to give the Hein Lectures for 1968.

I am even more grateful to students, to blacks, and to women, who are in the forefront of the movement for human liberation. They gave me some of the ideas and much of the inspiration.

My debt of gratitude to Gregory of Nyssa is far greater than any other. It was from him that I learned what freedom means. Nicolas Berdyaev and Vladimir Lossky led me to this seminal thinker of the fourth century who is so astoundingly contemporary.

This does not mean that I am not grateful to all my Western teachers. I learned certain ways of thinking from them, though not so well, I am sure. These teachers also goaded me to discover the Eastern tradition by their very ignorance of it—an ignorance which when coupled with a certain parochial smugness could not but elicit a strong reaction in a sensitive soul.

But that is not the attitude in which I submit these modest pages to my readers in both East and West. I offer here an invitation to dialogue, to experiment, and perhaps to achieve a true liberation of man in both East and West.

T. P. V.

Kottayam, India

Authority in Crisis

Ancient patterns of authority are fast breaking down. Anyone can see that. But the temptation is to bemoan this, rather than to understand what is happening.

Those of us who belong to the middle generation—the balding generation—are perhaps the most threatened. We are so threatened that we would do anything to shore up "law and order." As if that were more important than man himself! Yet, something is happening to us as human beings. Our crumbling structures have become both a threat and a call to fresh endeavor.

Children no longer obey parents. Wives do not submit to husbands. Employees are disobedient to their managers and employers. Are not the three basic relations of which the New Testament speaks all going to pieces? And now laymen do not obey priests or bishops. Students do not obey their teachers. Even soldiers are beginning to defy the commands of their officers.

Command is today the least effective way to make the other do one's will. One could try hidden persuasion or open bribery with much more effect, even in the home. One may coax with promises of reward or appeal to the other's sense of achievement, but command by authority is dying out everywhere.

Arbitrary command provokes only rebellion in most cases.

Good or bad? At least not so bad as we may think, I venture to suggest.

The same thing is happening in the field of faith or dogma. Once we used to believe things because the church told us so, or the Bible told us so. Now we want to know why one should or should not believe anything. We want to sift the evidence for ourselves and make up our own minds.

Judging by the results, there seems to be legitimate cause for some alarm. God dies for many. Ethical systems collapse almost completely. Nothing can be believed except what is the result of a scientific experiment. Man becomes dessicated and one-dimensional. Acquisitiveness and aggression reign supreme. If religion or the older generation had a little more authority, we could set some of these matters straight, some of us think.

This crisis of authority touches both the Christian church and human society at their very foundations. The church's dogmas and canons have long been overdue for revision. But mankind itself is groaning in deep pain, waiting for a new world to be born. Perhaps a fresh understanding of authority and freedom may hasten the process of that birth. It is in that hope that this volume is presented.

The argument in this book is that human growth is a process of which the central element is the dialectic between authority and freedom. All historical human existence is under some pressure to interiorize what is good in certain patterns of authority, to discard the older authority structure with all its freedom-hampering elements and to move on to a greater degree of freedom by developing new structures of authority that foster human freedom.

This judgment is based on certain presuppositions. First, that man is created good, and is meant to be the sum of all good. Second, that good that is compelled or forced is not really good, and therefore that freedom belongs to the very heart of the good. Third, that such a combination of freedom and the good is ultimately what we call love. But love itself needs certain structures within which to develop, which are the structures of a freedom-fostering community that embraces all mankind.

These are essentially Christian assumptions. But they can be tested in the life of man anywhere. This book is therefore not meant just for Christians. I hope it has a wider interest.

Chapter I is a sample survey of *some* contemporary patterns in the Western quest for an indubitable authority. All of these, the book submits, are bound to fail, because man is not expected to have an indubitable authority in historical existence. Even Christ is not such an authority who would tell one what to do or what to believe. The freedom of man is much too precious for that.

The Christian church has been much too authoritative and has too often failed to foster freedom. This accounts partly for the great contemporary reaction against authoritarian forms of Christianity and the rise of new forms of quasi religions which seek to embody some of the values of Christianity without accepting their foundation.

In Chapter II an attempt is made to delineate certain types of authority and freedom. Confusing these various types in ordinary discussion can lead only to various impasses in thinking. This chapter is quite lamentably sketchy, and open to severe objection by those who have come to regard Augustine as nearly infallible. The criticism of Augustine may not be justified by the facts. In that case, Western scholars could show us what those facts are. If, however, there is some truth in the criticism, Western theology would do well to take a second look at Augustinian thought.

In Chapter III we highlight the positive aspects of pragmatism, namely, the inseparability of knowledge and action; and we deplore the intellectual pseudomorphosis of Christianity. Here we refer to the Cappadocian theological concept that worship and ethics constitute the true setting for the knowledge of God rather than the conceptual grasp.

In Chapter IV we present a summary of one Christian's attempt to grasp the relationship between God, the world, and man. Gregory of Nyssa, despite his eclipse in Western intellectual life, seems still capable of correcting many of Augustine's deviations. He has a fresh and amazingly contemporary approach to the whole thing, except perhaps for the fact that human history plays but a limited part in his world view. But at least science and technology get better justice at his hands than at Augustine's. His conceptions of a dynamic universe and of the freedom of man still sound quite exciting. For him, authority can be an impediment to human growth, and he has grasped much more deeply than anyone else the Pauline insight that good enforced is not good at all.

In Chapter V we attempt to come back to the question of freedom in a contemporary context. A sketchy prognostication of the last third of the twentieth century is attempted in terms of the liberation of man. But this chapter became out of date as soon as it was written. The pace of liberation has been too fast for any writing to capture it in any up-to-date manner.

Chapter VI tries the impossible—to light a lamp to show the way forward. But people have to walk on this way for some distance before they can even be sure that this is the way forward.

The conclusion is simple. The way forward lies in hopeful, faithful, loving experiment. What is proposed here is merely the terms of the experiment, the equipment required for it, the question to be posed, the controls necessary. This book is not the answer. It is only an invitation to experiment.

Perhaps it is less—just an invitation to dialogue about an experiment. Maybe the experiment needs to be set up differently. My hope is that better minds than mine will apply themselves to the problems of freedom and authority—both within the church and in humanity as a whole—as well as to the negative deviations and false reactions in Christian thought.

The East needs the West just as much as the West needs the

East. The ecumenical movement has not yet broken through the middle wall. The intent of this book is not polemics, but provocation, an ancient pedagogic trick taken from the bag of Jesus.

But only one who loves can be permitted to provoke, even for the sake of communication. If that love is recognized, much in this book can be forgiven, and some of it can illuminate.

CHAPTER I

The New Quests

> Nowadays the great traditions of the Churches have often become nothing more than a futile attempt to restore their irrevocable past, side by side with a broad-minded adoption of all kinds of modern thought.
>
> —*Karl Jaspers*[1]

That was said in 1930, as a critique of the liberalism then prevailing in Christian thought. Despite the interregnum of Barth and Brunner, the situation is basically the same today.

The church is essentially uncertain about herself. She is not always taken seriously even by her own faithful. Official Christianity sounds so ludicrously unintelligent and seems so unappealing to the moral conscience of mankind, even to many who have not yet given up their Christian faith. Thus attempts are made here and there in the Western tradition, both in the churches and outside, to rehabilitate Christianity in a modern guise, or at least to find a significant alternative for it.

Here we shall deal with only five groups of related quests to modernize or supplant Christianity, indicated by slogans such as:

1. Secularization and pragmatism
2. The ontological disillusionment and existential stance

SECULARIZATION AND PRAGMATISM

The Concept of Secularization. No doubt secularization is a slogan. Yet it evokes many rich and varied thoughts. Once it meant the liberation of institutions and thought from ecclesiastical control. Today it means much more—among other things, an emphasis on the autonomy of man, a reaction against ontological patterns of thought, and a refusal to deal with any other world than the one which we now inhabit.

A very penetrating, though in some respects unsatisfactory, analysis of this movement in Western thought can be found in Carl Friedrich von Weizsäcker's Gifford Lectures of 1959–1960, published under the title, *The Relevance of Science.*[2]

Von Weizsäcker's book offers a brilliant historical analysis of the cosmogonical and cosmological speculations of man in myth and philosophy—although the book is quite limited when it comes to non-Western or patristic thought. He soon comes to Descartes, Newton, Leibniz, and Kant as the quartet that initiated our own "age of reason." The first three at least pretended that they "needed" God to explain the existence of the universe. Kant too "needed" God—but not for his universe known by "pure reason." It was only to explain the moral law within, not for the stars above, that Kant needed his God. The universe known to science (through our senses) is ultimately not the creation of God, but rather something produced by "the *a priori* forms of intuition and categories of the perceiving and knowing mind"[3] of man.

Here open secularization really begins, according to Von Weizsäcker. The argument from design for the existence of God was summarily dismissed by Kant. God is no longer a necessary appendage to the universe. Science is born, the umbilical cord which connected it with Christian civilization having been cut by the sharp razor of Kant's *Critique of Pure Reason.*

But God is not quite dead yet. For there is still that gap between the "physical" and the "organic" sciences where he can hide. Life cannot be explained by the "physicochemical laws of nature." Biology seems to deal with purposive existence, which it calls evolution—a directed process. Biology deals with the "history" of nature, not merely with its physicochemical description. There, in that purposive directedness, lies a slight but significant possibility to slip God in unawares. Bohr, Heisenberg, and Pauli are unwilling yet to assert that life can be explained by known physicochemical laws. Von Weizsäcker nods agreement, but then continues to ask: But when the laws that explain life become known, what else could they be but physicochemical laws? No, that gap can hardly hold God.

What about astronomy? Aren't there some gaps there where poor God could make a last ditch stand? As far as our little telescopes go (i.e., a mere one hundred million galaxies beyond our own) we find spiral nebulae, circular discs each containing some one hundred thousand million stars, most of them very ordinary stars like our own sun. But what lies beyond the one hundred million galaxies? Nobody knows at the moment. Our instruments are not powerful enough to find out. Can't we put God somewhere beyond the scope of our telescopes? We are all intelligent enough to know that that trick does not work either. Von Weizsäcker agrees with intelligent little you and me. The gaps of space cannot hold God.

What about time? Isn't that about the best "place" for us to put God—beyond time—in that "eternity"? Oh! blessed eternity—which no scientist can touch, since he is only concerned with the time-space universe! That looks like a fair ploy. "God who inhabiteth eternity"—that sounds much better than "God who dwelleth beyond space."

Besides, Von Weizsäcker tells us that he knows the age of the universe.[4] Somebody knows how much time there has been or when time began! The answer is $x.10^9$ years or, to put it in simple language, a few thousand million years.[5] I don't believe it, but the experts tell me that fifteen thousand million years is about the age of the oldest star around. (I don't know if some of the stars which were older died of old age or not.)

The universe is finite (the cosmic curvature of the Einstein hypothesis) and expanding at a measurable rate. So we can calculate when the big bang began which set the expansion going: exactly $x.10^9$ years ago, i.e., the same as the age of the oldest stars in the universe. So before that there was not time —only that thing which banged (what was that and where did it come from?). Von Weizsäcker does not think there is much to Fred Hoyle's continuous creation theory. It is simply an ingenious but conservative metaphysical hypothesis. It is empirically much more respectable to believe that the universe began at a given time, or that time began a given number of thousands of millions of years ago.

Science now believes it correct to say that the universe had a beginning in time, or as Augustine said, that the beginning of the universe is the beginning of time, and time has not been infinite.

It is therefore not legitimate to ask the questions: What was there before the universe began, and, Who caused the universe to be? Von Weizsäcker says that empirically both questions are meaningless because *unanswerable*. The scientist now becomes a dictator and tells us that we cannot put God in that gap beyond time. And reluctantly we have to agree that we cannot think of time beyond the beginning of time where we can put God.

So the "God of the gaps" is finally driven out of his last ditch. He vanishes into thin air. The world is ripe for "secularization."

Von Weizsäcker regards the contemporary world as "largely the result of a secularization of Christianity." [6] Science, to him, is the child of Christianity—an orphan child, he thinks. He cannot see how the notion of the "laws of nature," so fundamental to science, could have arisen from the Platonic under-

standing of matter as formless chaos. Science's notion of the
"law of nature" could have arisen only from the Christian doctrine of creation. God made matter, and God imposed upon
it certain laws which it unwaveringly obeys. It is in that belief
that science was born.

But science is no longer based on the notions that God made
matter and that God laid down certain laws which matter
has to obey. Before science came of age, the Christian
thought the world was finite, and that God was infinite. Later,
when God was dispensed with and secularization began, the
world became infinite, almost absolute. In our time the world
is again becoming finite, and secularization, which has been
settling down into a form of dogma, is itself becoming open
to reexamination. Absolutes are no longer affirmed. Everything is now relative, functional. Meaning can now be found
only in terms of the use and operation of things, not in terms
of their "being" or "substance."

Secularization itself, according to Von Weizsäcker, is a
largely ambivalent process. The dialectic within the medieval
catholic synthesis held together the conservative and radical
tendencies of Christianity in fruitful, living, mutual tensions.
Now that synthesis has broken apart. Secularization drove official Christianity into a conservative extreme, and the same
process wrenched the non-Christian world away from the
church into a radicalism which no longer remembers that its
values were drawn from Christianity.

But what is secularization? It is a secularized affirmation
of what Von Weizsäcker first expresses in traditional Christian
language:

> The gods of nature have been vanquished by the God
> whom Christians call Our Father; therefore man, as
> God's son, has received power over nature. As he is
> son and not servant, he is free, and his freedom in-
> cludes the freedom to act against the will of his
> Father, the God of love. He can now subject the world
> to himself, and secularism does precisely this.[7]

That is Gogarten's answer, developed by Von Weizsäcker.

Apart from the fact that it is much too Monophysite and perhaps unitarian in regarding God the Father, rather than Christ the God-Man, as the victor over the gods of nature, the statement quoted above is full of logical and theological difficulties and inadequacies. The above is as far as Von Weizsäcker went in this first series of lectures. He is neither a theologian nor a philosopher by training. It is as a scientist interested in philosophy and theology that he has spoken. We must respect his heroic effort to diagnose what is wrong with our age. But he himself would claim that his diagnosis is not final. I therefore suggest that, stimulated by him, we should move on to a more accurate diagnosis of our time.

Von Weizsäcker started his series of lectures with a more provocative and perhaps more profound set of statements:

1. Faith in science plays the role of the dominating religion of our time.
2. The relevance of science for our time can, in this moment of history, only be evaluated in terms that express an ambiguity.[8]

According to Western sociologists, a religion has to have a common faith, an organized church, and a code of behavior. Von Weizsäcker accepts this definition of a religion, which I know does not apply to the non-Christian religion I know best—namely, Hinduism, which has none of these three.

According to Von Weizsäcker, belief in science is the faith of modern secularism. The association of scientists is its priesthood, and the ability to use technical and mechanical apparatus its code of ethics. That certainly is an oversimplification. The rejection of the Christian knowledge of God and the Christian pattern of ethics, however, can in large part be explained by the fact that a new quasi religion has been on the rise in the West for the last three hundred years or so, which is imperceptibly replacing classical Western Christianity, which latter was itself a highly stylized and fundamentally altered form of the original faith of the church.

The current crisis for the knowledge of God and for Christian conduct is the consequence and symptom of Christianity's being challenged by a new religion. The crisis can be adequately faced only by a proper understanding of this new religion and by going back to the sources to recover the original genius of the Christian faith, for the new religion itself is a reaction against a distorted version of Christianity which has prevailed in the West ever since the sixth century.

The New Religion—American Pragmatism? The new religion of the West, it seems to me, is quite inarticulate and disorganized, without a clear dogma or body of belief. But then what is belief? We will let one of the high priests of the new religion speak:

> What . . . is belief? It is the demi-cadence which closes a musical phrase in the symphony of our intellectual life. We have seen that it has just three properties: First, it is something that we are aware of; Second, it appeases the irritation of doubt; and, third, it involves the establishment in our nature of a rule of action, or say for short, a *habit*. As it appeases the irritation of doubt, which is the motive for thinking, thought relaxes, and comes to rest for a moment when belief is reached. But, since belief is a rule for action, the application of which involves further doubt and further thought, at the same time that it is a stopping-place, it is also a new starting-place for thought. That is why I have permitted myself to call it thought at rest, although thought is essentially an action. The *final* upshot of thinking is the exercise of volition, and of this thought no longer forms a part; but belief is only a stadium of mental action, an effect upon our nature due to thought, which will influence future thinking. The essence of belief is the establishment of a habit, and different beliefs are distinguished by the different modes of action to which they give rise.

That was Charles Sanders Peirce, writing in the *Popular Science Monthly* in 1878.[9] And Peirce, that eminent exponent of pragmatism, is one of the clearest spokesmen for the new religion whose holy land is America. There are three prime elements in modern pragmatism, as enumerated by Morton White:

1. *Its hypotheticalism.* A statement can be tested for its truth value only if it can be translated unto a hypothetical form, i.e., an if-then form.
2. *Its operationalism.* A statement can be meaningful only if, in the hypothetical form of that statement, the "if" clause refers to a human operation, something that an experimenter does.
3. *Its experimentalism.* A statement can be tested for its truth value only if the "then" clause specifies some result which can be observed or experienced.

This is basically the methodology of science. It was Peirce who clarified it and made it a general principle applicable to all claims to truth. Peirce was not concerned about "truth" in its ontological or metaphysical sense. His interest was in "meaning"—that word being understood in a strictly operational sense.

What is reality for Peirce? Reality is that which is opposed to fiction or that which corresponds to a repeatable experiment producing the correct operational results every time.

In Peirce we see the close relation between faith, knowledge, and action. Faith itself is inseparably linked to knowledge. Faith is the passing over from uncertainty to certainty, the relaxation of thought from its straining to know, the rest to which the intellect returns after its quest.

But the rest is possible because knowledge has already charted the right course of action. The tension occurred not merely because of curiosity, but because of the need to know which operational pattern was best. In other words, faith itself is ethical—it is the restless quest to know what the right action is.

The pragmatic method has two consequences:

1. A trend away from deductive logic, from first principles and categories of reasoning, from necessities and axioms, toward things, their operational relations, their function, their end, their utility, consequences, and value.
2. A trend toward understanding truth itself, not in terms of that which *is* (the ontological view), but in terms of that which helps us to get into more satisfactory relation with other parts of our experience.

In other words, it is a wrong diagnosis of our time to see the new religion of the world as "scientism," "rationalism," "materialism," and so on. Its name, if name it we must, is "anti-rationalism," or "pragmatism."

Let us not erect the bogeyman of scientism, as many theologians are prone to do, and continue our worship of the scientific method by abjuring the demon of "scientism." The "scientific method" is but an aspect of our basic pragmatic orientation which consists in two propositions:

1. Meaningful knowledge is that which makes a difference in the way I deal with reality.
2. Meaningful conduct is that which affords me the satisfaction of a more rewarding relationship to the empirical reality which I experience.

These definitions of "the true" and "the good" are best exemplified in William James and John Dewey, two other great pragmatic pundits that America has produced. John Dewey put forward his main propositions thus:

> Judgments about values are judgments about the conditions and the results of experienced objects; judgments about that which should regulate the formation of our desires, affections and enjoyments.

Ethics is, then, the art of judging those things to be of value which have a relation in existence to what we like and enjoy. The choice is never between good and bad, but always between two goods. And their comparative merits can be ascertained only by knowing their respective relations to other goods.

This model of knowing and doing, i.e., the pragmatic, functional approach to truth and ethics, seems to be the heart of what I call, in no derogatory sense, the American philosophy of life. This in fact is the dynamic "new religion" spreading throughout the world. It is not rationalistic or materialistic. On the contrary, it is anti-intellectual, pragmatic, existential, this-worldly. This new religion is the true genius of the process we call secularization. It is essential that we approach this new religion without prejudice, to see what in it belongs to our heritage as Christians, and where the distortions are.

THE NEW RELIGION THAT FAILED—
THE ONTOLOGICAL DISILLUSIONMENT
AND THE EXISTENTIAL STANCE

The new religion of our time, American pragmatism, continues to be very much on the upswing. But it may come down with the collapse of the present economic pattern in the world, in which the West occupies a dominant position and is able continuously to produce and to appropriate more and more of the world's goods. The economic system of Western dominance is the matrix of pragmatism as a successful universal philosophy of success.

The understanding of the crisis of our time for knowledge and action may be helped by some knowledge of the other movement in Western spirituality, vaguely and incorrectly known as "existentialism." Here too, the movement was anti-intellectual, antisystematic, subjective. But it did not start out that way. Phenomenology and the search for a fundamental ontology, even when centered in the subjective, individual consciousness, were neither anti-intellectual nor unsystematic. Kierkegaard was anti-intellectual and antisystem. But he was only the father of modern existentialism. The mother was the phenomenology of Husserl and Heidegger. Husserl's quest was for intellectual certainty through careful mapping out of the whole region of consciousness. Heidegger's concern is primarily with "being"—not with "existence." He analyzed existential *Dasein* and propositional truth only as a step on the way to the analysis of "being" and "truth" as such. In other words both Husserl and Heidegger are primarily ontological in their orientation. Heidegger questions the assumption of "current" philosophy that truth is simply an adequate correlation between fact and proposition. For Heidegger, truth is a quality of being. And being is truth that transcends. His central question, "Why are there any beings rather than no being at all?" remains a challenge flung in the face of pragmatists and functionalists, which they continue to ignore.

For Heidegger truth is an openness, an "overtness," an *Erschlossenheit* of beings toward the being of man. This *discovery* or *unveiling* ("revelation") which is truth comes as a result of thought. Truth is a language event. Heidegger is thus not anti-intellectual. "Existence" for him does not mean what it means to Jaspers and many others—the ethical endeavor of man, in the context of his world, on behalf of his self. It means, rather, the position in which man stands outside the realm of concealment and asks the question, "Why is there any being rather than no being?" That is where human civilization began—in that stance and in that question. In other words, "truth" is neither in a correct proposition nor in the correspondence between fact and statement, but rather in that overt or open or unconcealed relationship of man to being, where he stands outside the realm of concealment, and allows "being" the freedom of being itself, i.e., of opening itself up to him. Truth is thus a relationship of unconcealedness between the knower and the known, not a correlation between fact and statement. But truth is also knowledge of *das Seiende im Ganzen,* of things in their totality of relationship, the knower himself included in that whole. Man's relationship, his *Gestimmtheit,* or "attunedness," to the whole is decisive for truth. That *Gestimmtheit* inescapably includes such elements as dread, anxiety, joy, sadness, and so on, and these affect the shape of truth in so far as they color the openness of man to being.

The openness of man to being or of being to man is of course not complete. The unconcealedness includes a measure of concealedness. All revelatory relationships simultaneously include openness and hiddenness. In this sense truth is never complete or final, and when it is taken as such, it becomes untruth. Thus truth must always include both the openness and the concealedness. When one of these is allowed to pass into oblivion it becomes untruth. Oblivion of what is unveiled as well as of what remains concealed, and error of judgment —these constitute two forms of untruth. The tendency to take a partial truth for the whole—a common ground of error —is but an aspect of the first form of untruth, namely, oblivion of what is veiled and what is unveiled. It seems to me that here Heidegger gives a good definition of heresy.

I have described this very un-American system of speculative reasoning in a great Western thinker simply to contrast it with American pragmatism. Heidegger leaves us in no doubt that his is no commonsense or ordinary language philosophy. In fact, Heidegger says so in so many words in his seminally important essay, *What Is Metaphysics?* Common sense and philosophy are opposed to each other by nature. Common sense clings to the facts and seeks one's own interests, forbidding questions that are inconvenient or difficult. Philosophy deals with a transcendent relationship in "existence," a relationship of openness and concealedness toward things in their totality of mutual relationships.

The pragmatist would immediately counter with the question: What difference does your philosophy make? If you cannot show us the pragmatic difference it makes, then it is meaningless.

To this Heidegger would answer that his question is the most momentous question that man can ask. It makes all the difference in the world to human existence and civilization, though it cannot be experimentally programmed to yield the hypothetical formula, "If X is done, then Y will follow."

It introduces and brings about an altogether new attitude of man towards his own life and all the things around him in the universe, owing to which he can know himself and the things in an "objective" way and can build up a historic world of civilization, guided by a sense of his position in the whole.[10]

To summarize then:

1. The dominant religion of the age is pragmatism rather than materialism or rationalism or scientism.
2. Secularization and pragmatism are correlated to each other and are behind the present crisis of authority in the Western world.
3. There are other alternatives to American pragmatism in the Western world, and Martin Heidegger represents one such significant alternative.

That other European ideology, vaguely organized under the term "the existential stance," will always have a function to fulfill in human thought. When it claims, however, to be a whole way of dealing with the problem of authority it misleads. The most existentially oriented of contemporary thinkers are themselves the products of tradition, even when they repudiate and react against that tradition as, for example, in the case of Sartre. Sartre is patently a European ex-Catholic. So is Heidegger a European ex-Christian. The existentialists have not escaped the problem of authority. They have only demonstrated that tradition can be authoritative in two ways —positively and negatively.

All of the three European forms of contemporary Western thought, phenomenology, existentialism and logical analysis, are searches for new ways of authenticating truth. They all have a common element—*the search for certainty through the search for the right method.* Modern philosophy as well as theology seeks authority in the *right method* of getting at truth. Is there a special method for theology? Or do we simply adopt the methods of contemporary secular thought? That is an important question to which we shall revert later.

"God's Death" and the Hermeneutical Quest

The "Death of God." William Robert Miller has provided us with an excellent anthology[11] of the "death of God" movement, which now seems to have passed its peak. The claim that Christianity has been superseded by something more "spiritually" advanced seems to have been constantly argued in the West, at least ever since the Enlightenment. Lessing (1729–1781) said that "Christianity has had its day." The French Revolution (1789) dethroned Christ in the West and sought to replace him with Reason. Sigmund Freud wrote about "the future of an illusion." Kierkegaard laughed at the ludicrousness of official bourgeois Christianity. By the beginning of this century, in Europe, once a solidly Christian continent, the majority had no formal continuing relation with the organized church, though many were still being baptized as Christians.

The dogmas of the church and her moral precepts were so widely debated, that it became obvious to many people that there were two sides to every issue. The majority chose the painless way of noncommitment. They were interested only in listening to broad liberal claims for values like education, progress, and social justice. A "nondogmatic affirmation of general kindliness and good fellowship, with an emphasis rather on the service of men than on the fulfillment of the will of God," became characteristic not only of European churches, but also of Rotary, Lions, Kiwanis, and other clubs in America and elsewhere.

The heroic efforts of the great neo-orthodox giants Barth

and Brunner have not, in the long perspective, sufficed to stem the tide. Only reason can dethrone reason, and Barth tried the big stick to scare reason away. A few Christians may have agreed to ignore reason for a while, but reason has proved herself bigger than the big stick of Barth.

Comfortable, middle-class Western Christianity, and some forms of authoritarian Christianity as well, seem no longer to count in the intellectual mainstream of the West. There was a conscious attempt on the part of a few young Western theologians to create a more radical form of Christianity. One could quickly mention a few converging contributions, beginning with Bonhoeffer's *Letters and Papers from Prison.* But there is a prehistory to this "new Christianity," which according to William Robert Miller begins with William Blake (1757–1827). Blake certainly was no pragmatist. On the contrary, he argued that if we had only the senses and reasoning power, we would simply "repeat the same dull round over again." It is the poetic and prophetic character of the mind that makes it possible for us to be genuinely creative. "The poetic genius" is the true man. It is poetic geniuses who create new religions, according to their differing cultural experiences and weaknesses. All religions are therefore essentially the same. Their point is liberation from the slavery of external rules by genuine inner creativity.

> And when he [Christ] Humbled himself to God
> Then descended the Cruel Rod
> If thou humblest thyself thou humblest me
> Thou also dwellst in Eternity
> Thou art a Man, God is no more
> Thy own humanity learn to adore.[12]

Yes, that is the heart of the thing:

> Thou art a Man, God is no more
> Thy own humanity learn to adore.

Then along came Schleiermacher out of German pietism, reducing the religion of "inwardness" to a psychological understanding of religion as *Gefühl* ("feeling") and *Erlebnis* ("inner experience"). No longer was there a need for a God "out there" or "up there," but God was very much "the beyond in our midst," in our hearts, in our feeling, in our experience.

When Nietzsche came on the scene, the Blakean notion of internal psychic energy and Schleiermacher's *Gefühl* became blended and transformed into the assertive will of man. Belief implies submission to power and authority, the loss of genuine human freedom. Christian dogma and Christian moral precepts are merely crutches for the weak. Dogmas and precepts survive because men need them to lean on.

But Nietzsche did not let Europe go with the mere charge of submissiveness. Tranquillity, passivity, and submission to authority soon provokes, according to Nietzsche, the reaction of restlessness, activism, and aggression. And Europe starts on its great evangelistic mission—that of enslaving others to its own slave morality.

Thomas Altizer, the most philosophically oriented of the "death of God" theologians, draws heavily on Blake and Nietzsche. Neither of these were atheists in the ordinary sense. Nietzsche's contention that God is dead is difficult to grasp. For he held, as Altizer and Hamilton have held, that the "death of God" is an event that took place recently.

If the world as we experience it is a creation of our minds and senses, then God was an actual component of that universe as man had previously perceived reality. But to Christian man this God became the terrible and mysterious power that stood over against him, judging and condemning him, a God "whose very sacrality is absolutely opposed to the life and immediacy of man's existence in the world." [13]

Or in Nietzsche's own more dramatic words:

> God degenerated into the contradiction of life, instead of being its transfiguration and eternal Yes! God as the declaration of war against life, against nature,

against the will to live! God—the formula for every lie
about the "beyond"! God—the deification of nothingness, the will to nothingness pronounced holy! [14]

It is this God whom Nietzsche's madman pronounced dead.
But, says Nietzsche, (European) mankind was not ready at
the end of the nineteenth century to hear the news of the
death of God:

> "There never was a greater event—and on account
> of it, all who are born after us belong to a higher his-
> tory than any history hitherto!" [15] Thus spoke the mad-
> man. His hearers . . . looked at him in surprise. . . .
> At last he threw his lantern on the ground, so that it
> broke in pieces and was extinguished. "I come too
> early," he then said, "I am not yet at the right time.
> This prodigious event is still on its way, and is trav-
> elling—it has not yet reached men's ears."

Our new theologians Thomas Altizer and William Hamilton
thought sixty years was about time enough to see if the world
was ready to hear the news of the death of God. They must
be just as disillusioned as Nietzsche's madman, despite first
impressions, seeing that the world of the last third of the
twentieth century is not very much more ready to hear this
news than was the Europe of the last decade of the nineteenth.

Yet, it is the pitiable parochialism in all this that should give
one pause. Is this the Christian God, the one who is so weakly
sovereign that he wants an enslaved humanity? Or does it
belong to a particular tradition of Europe—that of Augustine,
Luther, Calvin, and Barth? We shall seek to show in a later
chapter that there were significant alternatives in Christian
history to this jealous, petty, freedom-hating God, whom
Western civilization has created and now wants to murder,
but is not quite able to.

The Hermeneutical Quest. The mainstream of the Protestant tradition is not deeply impressed by the "death of God"

episode. Altizer's book *The Gospel of Christian Atheism* was criticized by Robert McAfee Brown as "not a gospel . . . not Christian . . . not atheism." Harvey Cox, author of *The Secular City,* has advanced what seems to be a more intelligent critique of the death of God movement. Altizer and Hamilton lack a sufficient eschatological horizon and that is what is usually wrong with liberal theologies. Cox, a good pragmatist, thinks "heaven" is still necessary as "the Copernican point of perspective from which renewal and insight emerge."

The mainstream of theology nowadays proceeds within narrow and manageable confines. Problems of being and becoming are usually beyond the theologians' competence. They prefer to take concrete questions such as: Who was the historical Jesus? What is the canon within the canon for interpreting the Bible?

Parallel to the secular man's quest for certainty, whether through the commonsense philosophy of pragmatism or the phenomenological speculative quest of Heidegger, and not uninfluenced by these, the hermeneutical quest of Protestant theologians proceeds.

While the pragmatist and the phenomenologist are following what they regard to be an infallible method, the Christian quest involves three realities—the man, the book, and the method. The method being sought for is to get at the authoritative man through the authoritative book. No commonsense method can help us understand the man or the book. We have to work hard at the analysis of the book through the form-critical and historical-critical methods in order to confront ourselves with the man Jesus as he was.

One school, led perhaps by Oscar Cullmann, thinks that we should take the whole Bible, i.e., as defined by the canon of the Old and New Testaments, as witness to salvation history, at the center of which stands the man Jesus. Another and more recent school, led by Ernst Käsemann, thinks that the book as a whole is not revelatory, and that we have to have a canon within the canon, like the principle of justification by faith, in order to understand the proclamation about the man Jesus in its central significance. Both schools stand in the Reformation tradition of *sola scriptura*. Both of them also imply that the basic revelatory event took place around two thousand years ago in the life of Jesus, and that God has *ceased* to perform *new* acts which are qualitatively of the same order as those witnessed to in the Bible.[16]

All such men affirm not only that a basic message or kerygma is contained in the Bible, but also that it is always obscured by later traditions of interpretation. The faithfulness of these later interpretations is to be tested by the original kerygma, and all one's labor is expended to get at this original kerygma. The interpretations are already in the Bible itself, and that is what makes the search for the original message so laborious.

Current disputes arising among the tradition-sifting hermeneutical investigators seem to relate to the question of the locus of this kerygma: Is it to be sought in the preaching of the post-Easter church, or in the self-consciousness of the pre-Easter Jesus? More recent investigators such as Richard R. Niebuhr, Wolfhart Pannenberg, and Jürgen Moltmann seem to insist on certain fundamental points:

1. No technique of historical investigation that *a priori* rules out the possibility of a physical resurrection of the body can do justice to the resurrection tradition that is central to the postresurrection kerygma.
2. When a pre-Easter Jesus without the resurrection is isolated from the post-Easter kerygma, it becomes impossible to account for the *fact* of the resurrection tradition which gave birth to the kerygma in the first place.

In other words, we are being brought back to the normal situation in which the evidence cannot by itself generate faith in the risen Lord. But the more arrogant claims made by users of the historical method to discredit the Biblical wit-

ness to the resurrection stand on a level with the mocking of
unbelievers such as the wise men of the Areopagus and philosophers like Celsus in the second century.

But the hermeneutical discussion within Protestantism has
not yet posed the fundamental questions of authority. For example, even when the historical-critical-archaeological investigation has finally unearthed the historical Jesus or the
kerygmatic Christ, whether pre- or post-Easter, are we not
confronted with the same choice as were the contemporaries
of Jesus and the apostles? Are we expecting the result of our
investigation to be authoritative to the unbeliever? Certainly
not. The hermeneutical quest seeks authority for the preaching
of the church and not for the faith of unbelievers.

But why preach Jesus? Why not preach "peace of mind"
or "love of neighbor"? Why not just preach "involvement in
history," as many contemporary preachers already do, following the pragmatic method, and not raising questions about
Jesus? Indeed, what is the authority for picking Jesus rather
than Socrates or Gandhi or Martin Luther King? If the answer
is, Because the Bible witnesses to Jesus, then we must ask
again: Why the Bible? What makes the Bible authoritative?

The current hermeneutical quest is thus not likely to yield
answers to the fundamental questions: How do I know God
and his universe? and, How do I mold my life? These are the
essential theological and ethical questions and they do not
seem to be tackled forthrightly by theologians.

And in the ecumenical dialogue there can be no other questions which are as primary as these. The current crisis for
Christian knowledge and action should drive us on to look
for a Christian epistemology that comprehends the pragmatic
and the phenomenological-speculative ways of knowing and
doing, and yet goes beyond them to what is specifically Christian in knowledge and action.

The smaller questions to which the hermeneutical quest
is currently addressed seem to be quite meaningless if the one
fundamental presupposition of the authority of the Bible is

itself in question. This is so not only for the unbeliever but for many a "conservative" Christian like the present writer, who seeks to be faithful to the authentic tradition, which never assumed the *sola scriptura* principle that the hermeneutical quest so naïvely presupposes.

THE FUTURE OF BELIEF AND BELIEF IN FUTURE

The Future of Belief. Parallel to the "honest-to-God," "death-of-God" tempests in the Protestant tradition, there has been a minor storm in Catholic circles over Leslie Dewart's *The Future of Belief.*[17] Dewart is too much of a Catholic to say that God is dead. He would simply "desupernaturalize" God by liberating our conception of God from its classical Greek moorings in static notions of "nature" and "being." The philosophy of Thomas Aquinas is metaphysical, and therefore "Greek" or Hellenistic. It uses the classical dialectic between two opposing principles, transcendence and immanence, in its conceptualization of God. His being is transcendent, his becoming is immanent.

The difficulty with this concept is not merely the insoluble academic questions it generates. It is irrelevant to the issues of life today. Modern unbelief is at least in part due to this irrelevance.

The "new life" which Christ brought, which is also called "grace," was opposed to the "old life" which it replaced. But the old was conceived in terms of a static nature. So the new was conceived, not as unnatural or nonnatural, but as supernatural. This "supernatural grace" was then conceived of as something totally unrelated to the world of nature—"an insubstantial ectoplasm flowing from above, a spiritual coin issued by God *ex opere operato* and certified as legal moral tender by the decrees of Providence." [18]

As the emphasis on supernatural grace grew, the immanence of God in the world came to be overlooked, and

God became more and more remote, no longer he who is present in the world and in man.

Too much of a gap between God and man makes God inaccessible.

> To sum up: the transcendence of the genuinely immanent God means this: if the God we find always *here* is not to vanish into thin air, if he is not to become an idol, if he is not to be reduced to the totality of being, and if he is not to be explained away as the becoming of the world or the projection of man—in a word, if the God who is actually *here* within being is the God of Christian tradition, it follows that he is not to be conceived as being.[19]

Dewart has been devastatingly criticized by his fellow Thomists, and enthusiastically welcomed by others both Catholic and Protestant.

He has been criticized by Fr. Bernard Lonergan for his faulty epistemology, or theory of knowledge, which seems to deny the validity of propositional truth as an adequation, or correspondence, between the knowing subject and the known object.

The present writer would venture the suggestion that much of Dr. Dewart's just criticism of classical Western theism would have been enriched by a knowledge of what the so-called Greek fathers actually said about the God-man-world relationship. This patristic view we shall sketch briefly in a later chapter.

Harvey Cox, who is an enthusiastic supporter of Dewart, criticizes him for not taking sufficiently into account the new eschatology, the hope in the future, now characteristic of much Marxist and liberal Protestant thinking. Let us say a word about "futurology" here.

Belief in Future. The future now becomes a substitute for the transcendent God. A spatially transcendent God is a quite difficult concept for Western thought. "Temporal transcendence," when depersonalized, can provide all the functions that

Harvey Cox wants from his heaven as a Copernican stance. And here the German Marxist philosopher Ernst Bloch shows the way in his monumental *Das Prinzip Hoffnung* (written between 1938 and 1949). Like Karl Barth, Bloch was an exile from Nazi Germany. His book was not published until 1959.

Bloch is an atheist and a Marxist by conviction, a Jew by origin and early training. As with Karl Marx, Jewish messianism shapes and influences his fundamental categories throughout. His *Principle of Hope* has created quite a stir in German intellectual circles, both Christian and Marxist. The avant-garde theologians of Germany today, as well as Harvey Cox of America, are all avid Blochists. Wolfhart Pannenberg, professor of systematic theology (Protestant) at the University of Munich, Johannes Metz, professor of fundamental theology (Catholic) at the University of Münster, and Jürgen Moltmann (Protestant) who taught recently at Duke University, the notable trio of German theology today, agree in commending Bloch as the new source (replacing Heidegger) of philosophical inspiration for Christian theological reflection.

For the atheist Bloch, the Bible is of central significance for mankind, in providing man with an eschatological consciousness. The prophetic movement in the Old Testament has set man on the way to living toward the future in expectancy and hope. Man as such is open toward the future. The new categories for his thinking are "possibility," "the new," "futurity," and the ontology of the "not-yet-being." [20]

Jürgen Moltmann's *Theology of Hope* follows this line of Bloch in a Christian context. Eschatology is the *logic* or science of the things to come at the end. But how can you have a science of things which have not yet come into being?

Christian eschatology is therefore not descriptive, but expressions of hope uttered on the basis of faith in the promises of God. It denies and negates the power of the present and the past in order to create a new future according to the promise. Hope thus contradicts experience, hoping against hope. The resurrection contradicted the cross. Hope contradicts the present shape of reality. The task of hope is to radicalize the tension between good and evil, between joy and suffering, between peace and war, between life and death, and to look to the absolute future of Christ for a universal and transcendent resolution of this discrepancy between what is and what ought to be. "With God all things are possible." The Christian hope is squarely based on the cross and resurrection. That is what distinguishes it from Bloch's *Hoffnung*. And it is to base hope on the cross and resurrection that these young German theologians have set about to reestablish the belief in the resurrection as a historical event. The hope of resurrection is based on the event. Without that hope we are in basic discontinuity with the primitive church. The resurrection of Christ is the firstfruits of the resurrection of man. Life beyond death and the hope for it belong to the essence of man, and where this is denied, man's being becomes stunted.

For these new theologians the resurrection of Christ is not merely a faith event or a *pro me* event as it was for Bultmann. It has universal significance for the whole of mankind. And this is the reason why these theologians are all the more anxious to be in dialogue with all men. Alas, they are inadequately equipped to converse with the majority of men in Asia, Africa, and Latin America, or even in the Latin countries of Europe. But they can hold conversations with their nearest cousins of the Jewish-Marxist heritage in Europe. And to this new Marxist element we shall now turn.

THE LIBERAL HUMANIST AND THE NEW MARXIST

Humanism, like socialism, is a generic concept. It includes all forms of thought in which man and the full development of his capacities are the central concern. Of course in general all humanists believe that the full development of man is possible and is to be sought and striven for.

The idea of development seems thus to be central to all forms of humanism. Today this notion plays a key role in secular thinking. The world itself is being classified into "developed" and "developing" nations. Economic development is regarded by most as the irreducible minimum of all development, and by many as the first stage in human development. But the difficulties of the notion of development itself become apparent when we consider what in addition to economic development should constitute the substance of human development.

In UNESCO discussions one hears two different terms often proposed—"spiritual" development and "cultural" development. But neither "spiritual" nor "cultural" can be unanimously or universally defined.

The liberal humanist today is committed to two things at least—the unity of mankind and faith in the future of man. But how to envisage that future and plan social engineering to achieve that future? That is where controversy begins. The liberal humanist conceives the future of man in somewhat simple terms—man should be peaceable, cultured, refined, interested in aesthetic enjoyment, in art and literature, in music and sports, and fairly comfortable and secure. There should be no violent upheavals, but by education and lawful change within a democratic structure we should be able to advance toward a just, peaceable, and creative society. There should be a pluralistic, permissive, tolerant social structure, allowing full play for all the human freedoms—of association, of opinion, of religion, of the press, of conscience, and so on. This is the kind of humanism that is implied in the United Nations Charter and the Universal Declaration of Human Rights—a lofty, gentle, benign, pleasant, refined, set of principles for universal application. Many of our intellectual leaders in the world subscribe, at least with the tops of their minds, to those worthy ideals, even when they find them difficult to practice in their private or public lives.

This liberal humanism has increasingly become the butt of ridicule and scorn at the hands of the more hot-blooded revolutionary thinkers, such as the political left wing in Latin

America, the Black Power leadership in the United States, and so on. The liberal humanist is accused of complacency and unwillingness to initiate radical change. His liberal ideas only help to give the glow of morality to a system that is basically corrupt and dehumanizing.

It is here that the Marxist humanist comes in both as a critic and as a pioneer. This is comparatively new even in Marxist circles, but it is the major indicator of vitality in European Marxism which is already becoming flabby and sluggish.

The developed Marx was himself rather averse to the line which later Marxists like Gorki and Rosa Luxemburg had once followed, namely the quest of the spiritual. Marx thought that any playing up of the religious and the spiritual would lead to unhealthy compromise with the establishment of religious reaction. The first priority was the economic emancipation of the proletariat. But now that such economic emancipation is more or less assured in many European countries, some Marxists are making bold to go behind the developed Marx to the younger Marx and his manuscripts of 1835–1847.

One of his earliest essays, written in high school (the Trier Gymnasium) in 1835, is published under the title "Reflections of a Youth on Choosing an Occupation." His guiding principle is "the welfare of humanity," and he insists that individual man can attain his fulfillment only by working for the benefit of the whole of humanity. His ideas while at the gymnasium and at the university seem to be the usual ones of Hegelian idealism. He was a baptized Christian, and though in touch with the development of radical Biblical criticism remained very positively disposed toward Christianity in its Hegelian version.

By the time he wrote his doctoral dissertation on "The Difference Between the Democritean and Epicurean Philosophy of Nature," he had turned against the God of Hegel and of the oppressive Prussian state. He turns away from the absolute state to the common people, from the ideal to the real, from the visionary to the pragmatic, or at least activist.

The shift from the ideal state to the principle of democracy led to the formulation that in democracy man does not exist for the state. Only when the democratic state is achieved will the alienated absolutist state wither away. The idea of political alienation soon leads to the idea of full human emancipation. Religion itself becomes an aspect of man's alienation from his own reality. Belief in God as a transcendent creator on whom man is dependent serves only to deny the significance of man. Atheism therefore is a necessary prelude to the affirmation of man.

But alienation continues to plague man. He works to create a political organization, wealth, and culture, but all three get out of his hand, and stand over against him as alien powers controlling his activities and enslaving him. In his 1844 manuscripts[21] Marx warns against "society" as an abstraction over against the real, concrete, human person as a social being.

This is the warning that many European Marxists are now beginning to take quite seriously. Erich Fromm has done us the great service of editing a series of such essays from European Marxists entitled *Socialist Humanism.*[22] Most of the writers are from the smaller socialist countries such as Yugoslavia and Czechoslovakia, where there is an agonizing reappraisal of what passes elsewhere for Marxist orthodoxy.

These writers emphasize one point—that man was the center of Marx's concern and therefore that anything that dehumanizes, whether in communist countries or in the West, is an enemy of man. Personal freedom is a value which cannot be subordinated to any collective interests. Strict planning destroys individual initiative and makes men the tools of the planners. Technological progress, if it dehumanizes, is not good. One generation cannot always be expected to sacrifice for the sake of future generations, especially if such sacrifice is decided upon by the ruling class and not by the people.

What does this new Marxism amount to in practice? It throws up as of first priority the questions: Who is man? What should he become in a technological civilization of the future?

How do we gain control of the dynamics of this technological civilization in order that it may become, in man's hands, a tool with which to forge his own future, rather than a threat to his free existence?

These are the questions of the time. Where do we look for an answer? To what authority will we appeal to find the correct answers? Bible? Church? Tradition?

One sees how utterly irrelevant much of our discussion on the authority for Christian knowledge and action is. Neither the bolstering up of Biblical authority by pseudoscientific criticism nor the refurbishing of the church's authority by some painless aggiornamento, nor even an adherence to tradition as something of the past can show us the way.

We have to seek and find the way, all the same.

CHAPTER II
Authority and Freedom

Authority and freedom are both words of imprecise meaning. This chapter seeks to clarify only some of these meanings.

TEN TYPES OF AUTHORITY

1. *Authority as Arbitrary Power Over Others.* This type of authority comes from a feudal society, in which the king, the emperor, or Caesar, had absolute authority to make other people conform to his will. In our own times, it is the dictator who typifies this kind of absolute sovereignty, i.e., the power to demand unquestioning obedience from his subjects.

One of the besetting errors of Christian thought has been to conceive of God's authority in these terms. Even today when we despise the man who seeks to exercise arbitrary authority, our theologians speak of the sovereignty of God as if it is always the case that God's task is to command and man's to obey. This destroys the dignity of both God and man, and we will have to come back to this point later on.

2. *Authority as Institutional Structure.* The clearest instance is the army. The centurion in Matthew's Gospel (ch. 8:9) says

to Christ, "I too am a man under authority, having soldiers under me." As an officer of the Roman army, he functioned within a clearly defined authority structure. He is under authority, he carries out the orders of his superiors. He also exercises authority: he can command his soldiers.

This hierarchy of command is very useful in a society organized for defense of the Roman Empire and its expansion. It was to be a mammoth tool of the Caesars. Individual freedom was not of much use within the army. Unquestioning and instantaneous obedience is what makes the army efficient.

Here authority, though arbitrary, becomes mitigated by being geared to a public purpose. But clearly when the military pattern of organization is extended to civil government or the administration of the church, it becomes totally vitiated. Yet the temptation seems always to be there.

3. *Authority to Do Particular Things.* Here we can imagine the authority of government officials (police, tax collectors, or magistrates) as well as authority of ordained ministers of the church (preaching, administration of the sacraments, etc.). In this latter case, it would be a basic misunderstanding of ministerial authority in the church to compare it with civil authority, and to see the priesthood primarily in terms of authority.

4. *Authority for Truth.* When I say, "I can tell you on the best available authority that the earth came into being *x* million years ago," I use the word "authority" to mean something other than the capacity to do or to make others obey. I mean that I have not personally examined the evidence for the statement and am perhaps not quite competent to judge its adequacy. But those who have done so, who have the knowledge and competence necessary for it, and whose judgments are generally reliable, tell me that such and such is the case. I accept their judgment, at least tentatively, until I am told otherwise on better authority. Most of our knowledge is

of that kind. How do I know that the earth moves in an orbit about ninety-three million miles distant from the sun or that the population of India is more than five hundred million? I have neither measured nor counted these myself. In fact, a great deal of education consists in accepting knowledge that is the result of other people's investigations.

5. *The Authority of Experience.* This is the kind of authority which is most convincing to the rational mind. In science it is the experimental method which is the basic source of authority, though science cannot be understood simply as the gathering of knowledge by experiments.

But even in the matter of experience, a distinction should be made between private experience and a repeatable, demonstrable, public experience. The authority of private experience does not have compelling authority except for the one who experiences it. But both in private experience and public experiments, there is a chain of reasoning which interprets the meaning and significance of the event. Experience by itself is not authoritative, but only in combination with logical reasoning and the clarification of alternative possibilities. We should not say that experience has any authority apart from its interpretation. But it is one thing to question the facticity of the experience and another to challenge its interpretation. Both the facticity of the event and the validity of the interpretation are necessary to establish the authority of experience. (This is particularly true in the case of the cross and resurrection.)

6. *The Authority of Persuasion.* Persuasion has been recognized from early times to be one of the most effective sources of power. The demagogues and rhetoricians of history were those who had developed the capacity to make other people do what they wanted by appealing to reason and emotion. Persuasion has never really been a fully rational process. Some of the basest emotions of men, as well as some

of the noblest, were often appealed to. Even today the advertising industry specializes in this kind of persuasion. Persuasion is more authoritative when it is hidden.

7. *The Authority of the Collective.* There are certain socially accepted ways of believing and behaving which become the "right" thing to do, even when they have no essential rationale behind them. "Keeping up with the Joneses" is a clear case of the authority of the collective. Thus are many convictions and beliefs acquired from our general concourse with fellow members of our society, in school, college, or adult life. Sometimes it is a particular class that is authoritative. At other times, it is a religious or political institution that determines our values and beliefs.

8. *The Authority of "Success."* In our competitive societies, success itself gives authority. The Japanese, for example, at the end of the Second World War were willing to reject many of their own cultural values and adopt many Western values, primarily because they had "failed" and the Americans had succeeded. This accounts also for the authority of a sports or movie star in matters of politics or economics.

9. *The Authority of Tradition.* Certain mores and values are inherited from our forefathers and often acquire a peculiar sanctity on account of their antiquity. Tradition is the way in which a community is conditioned to think, to act, and to worship. It is closely tied up with the community's historical identity. Many of our religious and cultural practices and beliefs derive their authority primarily from tradition.

10. *The Authority of Sanctity of Personality.* Especially in Oriental societies, though not only in them, one finds that a sanctified or holy man of God commands great respect, and his authority in many matters is at least theoretically recognized. Mahatma Gandhi of India was clearly such a case.

His authority did not come from any official position he had or from his capacities for persuasion. To a lesser degree, Albert Schweitzer used to wield some such authority for the West, though admiration rather than emulation was also the usual Western response to him.

This list was not meant to be exhaustive, but was intended to show the variety of meanings the word has. And there are other types of authority to which we need to refer here, which are of particular importance in the sphere of religion.

The authority of a book, or scribal authority. All the great religions of the world have one or more books which they regard as authoritative. The Old Testament for the Jew, the Quran for the Muslim, the Bible for the Christian, the Vedas and the Upanishads for the Hindu, the Zend-Avesta for the Zoroastrian, the Dhammapada for the Buddhist. Even modern religionists such as the Mormons and the Christian Scientists have their "scriptures" that are held in high respect as unique books, uniquely authoritative. Usually there is an official class of interpreters of the Scripture, the scribes of the Jews being a clear example.

The authority of spiritual power. All religions recount some heroic or miraculous acts of their founder that demonstrate his spiritual power and his direct contact with God. The religious leader wielded personal authority, not merely because of the sanctity of his personal life, but by his charismatic personality, which demonstrated extraordinary power not available to ordinary men. This was true not only of the founders of religions, but also of their propagators. The lives of the apostles, as well as of later Christian missionaries who evangelized other parts of the world, are full of miracle stories, even as late as the nineteenth and twentieth centuries.

Religion does not spread by ordinary authority of persuasion or arbitrary power, though these have often helped immensely. Even the theme of sanctity of life has not been the most immediately effective source of the dynamic of religious expansion. The element most lacking in all religions today is the

numinous, extraordinary, charismatic power which carries conviction neither by compulsion nor by persuasion.

Jesus himself is witnessed to as having exercised this authority both in his teaching and in his dealing with men. It was
never simply a question of miracles. Matthew's Gospel (ch.
7:29) says, "He taught them as one who had authority, and
not as their scribes."

In other words, authority was a combination of the authority
of the Scriptures and that of the official magisterium, which
taught according to certain set rules of hermeneutics or ex-
egesis. This is the kind of authority still exercised in the Christian church, with less and less effect. The Bible and the
hierarchy, or the Bible and the professor (or pastor), belongs
to the first type of authority—the authority of the book and
its official interpreter.

Jesus' authority seems to have been self-authenticating,
though by no means irresistible. He taught with authority
(*exousia*). He acted with authority in forgiving sins and casting out demons.[23] He was not a slave to the book or to the
rules, but he discerned and decided what was right, taught it,
and did it. His authority was a free authority, not an aspect of
hierarchical authority. His freedom was also his authority.

The Dialectic of Freedom and Authority

The dialectic between authority and freedom is a delicate
one to unravel. Only in the case of arbitrary authority can we
say that authority on the part of the commander is opposed to
freedom on the part of the one who has to obey, whether he
be slave, soldier, or religious addict. Arbitrary authority uses
the other will (of the one who obeys) as an extension of its
own will and thus denies all freedom to it. The other will is
simply a tool or an instrument, to be used according to the
will of the commander.

In persuasive authority, however, an appeal is made to the
other will to exercise its freedom to initiate its own action in

the direction proposed by the persuader. The other will has to respond in freedom, not merely give unquestioning compliance. The difference between demagoguery and true persuasion is that the latter respects the autonomy of the will of the other. Only persuasive authority can genuinely foster freedom in the mature.

Alfred North Whitehead, that great American savant, often draws our attention[24] to the great insight of Plato in his more mature years, i.e., in the *Sophist* and in the *Timaeus,* that the divine element in the world is a persuasive agency and not a coercive one. Whitehead says, "This doctrine should be looked upon as one of the greatest intellectual discoveries of the history of religion."

What Whitehead means is that only a God who uses persuasive authority would be respecting the freedom and dignity of man. Perhaps he found the Puritan God of early New England a bit too overbearing. That God was still the God of the Old Testament, the one who thunders. There is something very arbitrary about Yahweh. He certainly was no mild and persuasive agency. When he gave the Ten Commandments, did he try to persuade the people of Israel with reasonable arguments why it was philosophically untenable, or not in the best interests of man, to murder or bear false witness? Did he not rather shout: "I am Yahweh your God. Therefore you shall not . . . "? When Yahweh demanded from Abraham the sacrifice of his only son, the son of promise, did he try to persuade Abraham by gently disclosing the reasons why he made that demand?

Job wanted to have a persuading God, a God ready to debate, with whom he could argue dispassionately about justice in the world. (Job 23:3 ff.) But when God actually appears, he is arbitrary, he commands, he questions, but he does not persuade. All Job can do is to forget about the debate, and repent in dust and ashes (ch. 42:5–6).

Neither would Luther nor Calvin have conceived a mild and persuasive God—especially not Luther. His is the God who thunders and sends forth lightning. He makes the mountain smoke and burn. When the sound of the trumpet blows loud and strong, who can stand in the presence of Yahweh without fear and trembling?

Whitehead's remark about Plato's insight would hardly apply to the God of the Old Testament. But how would it fare in the case of the God and Father of our Lord Jesus Christ?

Apparently Kierkegaard did not like the benign God in Hegel. He wanted to reinstate the scaring God of the Old Testament. Faith is generated only in the context of an unreasonable demand from God, as in the case of Abraham. In fact, God's demand is so arbitrary that it not only suspends the ethical, but even contradicts his own perpetual commandment, "You shall not kill." Martin Buber criticizes Kierkegaard for relativizing the ethical by the latter's unqualified praise of Abraham going to sacrifice his young son in response to a demand from God.[25] Kierkegaard would reply that what God demands is the ethical, and that God's demand cannot be evaluated by some extraneous absolute ethical norm.

But is not the absolute ethical norm, "Thou shalt not kill," also instituted by God? Is not God demanding disobedience by making two contradictory commands? Kierkegaard would reply that it is the sovereign God who lays down the general ethical norm and who demands the "teleological suspension of the ethical" in a particular context, and therefore that obedience has to be rendered in the context. It is not to everyone that God makes a demand that goes beyond the absolute norm. Only the "single one," the chosen one, is so isolated and tested.

That kind of contextualism leaves many questions unanswered. How am I to know for sure that the demand for the teleological suspension of the ethical comes from God, and not from my own passions and desires? How am I to recognize the voice of God amidst the cacophonic medley of voices that is the twentieth century? If, for example, the revolution demands that in the teleological perspective of the welfare of man, I should murder my fellowman, can I take it to be the same voice of God that spoke to Abraham and demanded the slaughter of his well-beloved, only son?

On the one hand, I must confess, there is something of the Nazi in all of us. We want an arbitrary dictator as our God. We admire naked and irresponsible power, albeit secretly. That perhaps was the secret of the great influence that Barth once had. But then sooner or later, and often sooner than later, the reaction sets in. We find this arbitrary God too much of a meddler, as the Roman people invariably found their Caesars to be. Then we plot to murder our God by downright atheism or "Christian atheism."

The problem of the authority of God is the problem of the freedom of man. It is when we find human freedom leading us into evil, as it did in the case of Nazi Germany, that we immediately invoke an arbitrary God who denies freedom to man. Thus we seek to escape responsibility by laying down our freedom and making God a slave driver. If not God, perhaps de Gaulle . . . !

Freedom and the Individual

Perhaps by far the most serious deviation in classical Western Christian theology is the underplaying of man, his dignity and his freedom. Here a major share of the responsibility goes to Augustine—that amazing fountainhead and towering genius of the Western intellectual tradition, both Christian and secular.

Augustine is not a doctor of the universal church. Let us make that quite clear. The Eastern tradition has consistently refused to take his views as suitable for Christian teaching—though many of these did infiltrate into that tradition, but never under his name. He is neither father nor doctor for the Eastern church. Not that we regard him as a heretic, nor do we minimize his spiritual and intellectual achievements. It is simply that he does not teach within the authentic tradition. His innovations are often misleading. And his understanding of man as totally sinful, without any capacity for good in him, could be understood only as a pious confession of human frailty, but not as a matter of faith to be taken completely seriously.

We should, of course, understand Augustine in his context, in order to do him justice. His fundamental preoccupation, from his very youth, was with the problem of evil—evil in the world, evil in the self. That was the central question in a distintegrating Roman Empire. The philosophers and the theorists wrote in praise of reason and freedom, the classical values of Hellenic civilization. But the reality of the Greco-Roman Empire of the fourth century was that it was crumbling, mainly due to moral evil—lack of moral fiber in the emperors, the prefects, the guards, the senators, the people. The will of man had gone flabby and wicked, sensuous and aggressive. It was in the will that evil was regnant. But whence this evil?

There were two answers readily available, and Augustine tried Manichaeism first. Mani (ca. 215–275) was a Persian philosopher who taught a kind of Bahaism that was popular among intellectuals. Manichaeism was a liberal religion which regarded Jesus, the Buddha, the prophets, and Mani himself, as men sent by the Lord of light to liberate the original particles of light which Satan had stolen from the kingdom of light and later hidden in the evil human body.

Satan himself, according to Mani, was an eternal principle of evil—an evil God of darkness opposed to the good God of light. Release of the good in us would come through ascetic practices and even vegetarianism. Augustine tried it for nine years. No good particles of light seemed to have been released from his body—until the grace of God came in Christ.

There and then he decided two things. First, there are no particles of light hidden in man. If man is to be good, the good has to come from outside, by the grace of God, by the hearing of the Word, by baptism. Man is totally evil. And there is no second God of evil.

In his earlier works as a Christian, Augustine is most concerned to defend the sovereignty of God over against a second god of evil, and to find the source of evil somewhere else than in the good God.

There the second answer—that of the Cappadocian fathers, which he got either through Jerome and Ruffinus or through Ambrose—came to his aid. Gregory Nazianzen (329–389) had clearly taught:

> Believe that evil has neither substance nor kingdom, whether unoriginate or self-existent or created by God; it is our work and that of the evil one, which befell us by heedlessness, but not from our Creator.[26]

His colleague Gregory of Nyssa had put it even more explicitly:

> No growth of evil had its beginning in God's will. Vice should have been blameless were it inscribed with the name of God as its maker and Father. But evil is, in some way or other, engendered from within, springing up in the will at that moment when there is a retrocession of the soul from the good.[27]

Nyssa had clearly stated, in the same work, that evil springs from human freedom—that God did not make man do evil, but that man did it of his own free will. But evil has no substance. It is the lack of good. It is an eclipse of the good—a shadow.

Augustine also takes over the Cappadocian argument against the evil God of the Manichaeans. Evil is finite. If this God is capable only of evil and not of good, then he is not free. Therefore he is neither God nor eternal.

Having thus denied an unoriginate eternal principle of evil, Augustine had to speak of the free will of man in order to explain the origin of evil. But in this later controversy with the

Pelagians, some of these anti-Manichaean writings on free will were used by his enemies against his own doctrine of grace. Hence his withdrawal, toward the end, of the emphasis on free will [28] and his settling down to regard human freedom as a neutral, medium kind of good, not central to human nature.

Unfortunately, on the other hand, he regards evil itself as central to human nature. For had he not fought with all the Manichaean weapons against concupiscence in his own soul, only to see himself fall again and again, evil having been ineradicably entrenched in his nature? Evil lies in *natura mea*.

The whole of humanity is a *massa damnata*, a lump of sin out of which no movement toward the good can come. The vaunted virtues of Hellenic philosophy—reason and freedom —are themselves in bondage to sin. Desire precedes thought. The will goes before the mind, deflecting and distorting it. *Partum mentis praecedit appetitus.* It is love that decides which way the mind goes. Love has only two choices— Jerusalem, city of God (heaven), or Babylon, city of the earth (the crumbling Roman Empire). *Natura mea* inclines me always to Babylon, the worldly city, the secular city. Only the grace of God coming from outside the *massa damnata* can lift my love up to Jerusalem.

Augustine thus dramatized what is an authentic Biblical insight:

> The desires of the flesh are against the Spirit, and the desires of the Spirit are against the flesh; for these are opposed to each other, to prevent you from doing what you would. (Gal. 5:17.)

In overdramatizing these words of Paul, however, Augustine laid the foundations for an idea deeply entrenched in Western culture—the idea that evil or sin is an integral part of human nature. What was a phenomenological observation in Paul is made ontological in Augustine. For Paul, sin is an enemy that has come into humanity from outside.[29] We are freed from sin by Christ, and are not to yield ourselves to it, says Paul.[30]

For Augustine it becomes a central reality and a basic pre-occupation.

It may be useful, even if presumptuous, to see where the basic distortions of Christian teaching that stem from Augustine impinge upon us today. If the following remarks appear too sweeping in relation to Augustine, it would still be useful to acknowledge that they are real deviations.

FIVE DISTORTIONS

1. *A Low View of the Incarnation.* Augustine's Manichaean background shows through in his incapacity to take the flesh of our Lord sufficiently seriously. Monophysitism and Manichaeism are country cousins, and the one usually brings the other along. Regard the flesh, the body, matter, as evil, or even inferior, and one has already begun the deviation from Christian truth.

When Augustine says, for example, about our looking at Christ, that "it is better that you do not see this flesh, but picture to yourself the divinity," [31] he is probably not a monophysite, and is simply following an early line of Athanasius. But the following quotation, which could be duplicated, reveals a deeper distrust of the flesh, of the world, of existence-in-time, and therefore of the incarnation itself:

> There is one thing that is transitory in the Lord, another which is enduring. What is transitory is the Virgin birth, the Incarnation of the Word, the gradation of ages, the exhibition of miracles, the endurance of sufferings, death, resurrection, the ascent into heaven —all this is transitory. . . . Whoever desire to understand God the Word, let not flesh suffice them, because for their sakes the Word was made flesh, that they might be nourished with milk.[32]

This playing down of the incarnation is at the root of many problems in contemporary theology, including its overly eschatological orientation. Even the new theology of hope is based on a *promise,* as in the Old Testament, not on the fact of the incarnation, which is the true starting point of the Christian faith.

2. *Flight from the World.* As a consequence of his low view of the incarnation, Augustine undervalues this world. Or the converse might be the case. This comes out most clearly in the radical polarity he poses between Jerusalem, the city of God, and Babylon, the city of the earth. Babylon is the creation of sinful man in his love of the world. It is the flowing river of time where nothing is permanent. It is something to escape from, for

> it flows . . . it glides on, beware, for it carries things away with it.

But Jerusalem is otherwise:

> O holy Sion, where all stands firm and nothing flows!
> Who has thrown us headlong into this [Babylon]?
> Why have we left thy Founder and thy society? Be-
> hold, set where all things are flowing and gliding
> away, scarce one, if he can grasp a tree, shall be
> snatched from the river and escape. Humbling our-
> selves, therefore, in our captivity, let us "sit upon the
> rivers of Babylon," let us not dare to plunge into
> those rivers, or to be proud and lifted up in the evil
> and sadness of our capacity, but let us sit, and so
> weep.[33]

That attitude is precisely what modern theology reacts against. We cannot refuse today to plunge into the flowing waters of time, there to be involved in the torrents of politics and economics, of race and war, of all that touches the welfare of man. The incarnation has taken place in this Babylon. Jeru-salem is here, at the very heart of Babylon. We cannot escape into a heavenly and static Jerusalem, however much we may be scared of the flowing stream of time. In fact, the church is the place of abiding in the midst of the torrent, the Jerusalem in the midst of Babylon.

Augustine's idea of the two cities comes up in the Western tradition in various ways—nature and supernature, nature and grace, world and church, law and gospel, the two kingdoms of Luther, reason and revelation, and so on.

It is this basic dualism and the failure to regard the two as interpenetrating, that has caused much of today's secular reaction. Modern man refuses to accept a flight from the world of time into the unchanging immobility of a static heaven.

3. *Man as Abject Dependent.* Because Augustine is tempted to regard Christ's humanity as but a means, an instrument, a vehicle, and not as something permanent and valuable in itself, he is able to have a *low view of man.* Only if we remember that it is a Man who sits at the right hand of the Father as Lord of all, can we have an adequately high view of the new humanity. This Augustine is unwilling to accept. Man still can do nothing of himself. Whatever he does on his own is for that very reason wrong and sinful:

> Man is not anything of such kind that, having come into being, he can as of himself do anything rightly, if He who made him withdraws Himself from him, but his whole good action is to turn to Him by whom he was made, and to be made just by him, and pious and wise and happy.[34]

This childish dependence of man on God is what Nietzsche caricatured as the slave morality. It is an affront to human dignity, and certainly not the view that Christ and the apostles hold about man. The "world come of age" cannot brook this insult to mankind. It is not the Christian Gospel which undermines man in order to exalt God. It is too petty a God who can have glory only at the expense of the glory of man. The Augustinian ideal of man as God wants him is a beggar:

> A beggar is he who ascribeth nothing to himself, who hopeth all from God's mercy. Before the Lord's gate he crieth every day, knocking, that it may be opened unto him, naked and trembling, that he may

be clothed, casting down his eyes to the ground, beating his breast. This Beggar, this poor man, this humble man, God hath greatly helped. . . .

The assumption of polarity between the interests of God and those of man is perhaps responsible for the reactions of "secular theology" and "death of God" theology.

4. *Emphasis on Individual Salvation.* Augustine's soteriology was focused too strongly on *the individual man* and *his deliverance from personal sin* (original and actual). Sin was further misunderstood as primarily located in concupiscence, the love of Babylon, the city of earth. (Of course, Augustine was not an "individualist." He has much to say about the body of Christ and about the corporate character of the heavenly Jerusalem, the church.)

This soteriology leads to two errors. First, by concentrating on individual sin, it takes our eyes off the evil entrenched in society itself. If only individuals are to be plucked out from the flowing stream of time and placed on the safe rock of Jerusalem, then the campaign against social injustice has very little significance. But if the kingdom of God has to be manifested in human history, then there has to be something more than individual saints. Society itself has to be "saved."

Second, by concentrating on salvation from sin, we are caught in a negative view of salvation. The "image of God" view of salvation, as taught in the Eastern tradition, makes the demand that the unlimited goodness of God has to be concretely manifested through the corporate righteousness of man on earth. Our secular theology moves away from individual and otherworldly holiness, to a corporate and this-worldly holiness.

Perhaps we are overdoing this denial of personal holiness and otherworldly sanctity. We need, however, to recover from a one-sided view of salvation as merely the deliverance of the individual from his sin. We need today a positive view of salvation which uses human freedom to discern and create new forms of social and personal good.

5. *A Low View of the Sacraments.* As has already been implied, Augustine's devaluation of the body, and therefore of matter, is reflected in his low view of the sacraments.

> Leave them abroad both thy clothing and thy flesh, descend into thyself, go to thy secret chamber, thy mind. If thou be far from thine own self, how canst thou draw near unto God? For not in the body but in the mind was man made in the image of God.[35]

Gregory of Nyssa, as we shall see later, would not agree that the body has nothing to do with the image of God. This underplaying of the sacraments as *verbum visibile,* an accommodation to our weak bodily nature, of the pure Word, which must be invisible, has Manichaean antecedents.

Without the recovery of a richer sacramental view, we cannot recover a theology that takes the incarnation seriously. The world is good, the body is good. Without the body, there are no senses; without the senses, the human mind knows nothing. Christ has taken his body into heaven. Matter is the medium of the spirit. In fact, matter itself is spiritual—so the Eastern fathers would argue.

If theology is to do justice to technology and culture, a higher view of the sacraments is necessary. But this is not the place for an elaborate excursus on the topic, for the very word *sacramentum* is alien to the Eastern tradition.

These five fundamental deviations which have their origin in Augustine are pointed out, not to show the superiority of one tradition over the other, but in order that we may all correct each other and be corrected by the authentic tradition. We started on this line with a discussion of Augustine's great fear of freedom. But behind that fear lies a deeper failure— the failure to understand man as made in the image of God. No adequate solution to the problems of authority and freedom can be discerned until the meaning of the image is more fully grasped.

CHAPTER III
Deviations and Distortions

It is quite easy to assume that some form of authority is necessary for man, and then to proceed with the question, Which authority? Here we need to question the assumption itself. For behind the very notion of authority there lies Kierkegaard's vexing question of the "starting point."

If I say that I believe in Jesus Christ, someone may very well ask me, On what authority? I may answer either, For the Bible tells me so, or, The church tells me so. This can provoke a further question: On whose authority do you believe the Bible or the church? And the series can be carried on ad infinitum.

If on the other hand I say, Because I have experienced that Jesus Christ delivers me from the power of sin, I am resorting for my authority to a private experience that cannot be checked publicly and cannot therefore serve as authority for anyone else. The same is the case if I say, Because the Holy Spirit convinces me inwardly that the testimony of the Bible is true.

Another possibility is brazenly to argue for the immediate authority of the pragmatic method, as Barbara Ward ingeniously does in her book *Faith and Freedom.*

> Since . . . the Western mind has in the last century
> become more and more accustomed to think of proof

in the pragmatic terms of modern science—a thing being "true" if it can be shown to work—it is perhaps worth remembering that even here in the sphere of pragmatic proof faith and science conform to a similar pattern and claim a comparable validity.

Miss Ward puts the following words into the mouth of the "Saint":

> We, the scientists of goodness, tell you that if you will take the raw materials of your all too human mind and body and process them through the laboratory of detachment, humility, prayer, and neighborly love, the result will be the explosion into your life of the overwhelming love and knowledge of God. Do not think that you can know God except by hearsay unless you submit yourself to this experimental process, any more than you can produce nuclear fission without an Oak Ridge or a Harwell. But we promise that if the experiment is carried out under clinically pure conditions— as it has been in the life of the best and purest of mankind—then the result is scientifically certain. The pure of heart shall see God. That statement of fact is as experimentally certain as that H_2O is the constitution of water, and it is proved by the same experimental means.[36]

Coming from a Roman Catholic, this is surprising. The argument does not invoke the authority of magisterium or tradition. And it raises two questions: (*a*) What happens to the doctrine of "prevenient grace" necessary for faith? Is this not too Pelagian? Can we, simply by doing certain things, force the vision of God? Can the vision of God too be reduced to an if/then formula? Or is it a free gift? (*b*) Are we reducing God to the level of the Q.E.D. ("that which was to be demonstrated") of a laboratory experiment, thereby bringing him within man's controlling power?

There is a point of great significance, however, in the lady's words. Her basic intuition is right, that the theoretical-cognitive is inseparable from the practical-ethical-cultic. That separation has taken place in our Christian history, and the current crisis is at least in part the consequence of this breach between the cognitive and the ethical-cultic.

But the breach took place ages ago. However much we may disagree with Harnack's analysis of the development of dogma as a basic distortion of the church's spirituality, we have to concede that the overdevelopment of theology and speculative philosophy in the Christian West can at least in part be attributed to the alienation of thought from life and worship.

THE PSEUDOMORPHOSIS OF CHRISTIANITY

The second century of our era already witnesses to this *pseudomorphosis*. It was not so much in the writings of the Apologists, who tried to accommodate Christian truth to Greek philosophy, but more in those who fought against heresy—particularly against the Gnostic and Arian heresies—that the undue emphasis on "right teaching" began to go on a dangerous deviation.

Pseudomorphosis is a term which comes from mineralogy. Different elements in crystallizing assume varying geometrical shapes—sphere, cube, cone, and so on. It is observed that such crystals of various minerals are seen in the rocks. Imagine one of these crystals disintegrating in the course of time, leaving an empty space in the rock, say in the form of a cone. Into this empty space later on comes a solution of another mineral which normally crystallizes as a cube. But it has only the space of the cone available to it. So, contrary to its "nature," it takes a conical shape. This is pseudomorphosis. Spengler draws our attention to this phenomenon occurring also in the field of values and ideals.

It is possible to argue, with Leslie Dewart, that Christianity underwent something of a pseudomorphosis in the second, third, and fourth centuries. But the process was not a simple assimilation of Hellenistic categories by Christian apologetics or theology.

In the struggle against the Gnostic heresy, Irenaeus developed the notion of apostolic succession for the right teaching, a notion first advanced by the Gnostics themselves.[37] But the particular brand of Gnosticism against which Irenaeus was contending had itself undergone a pseudomorphosis.

The Gnostic tradition had its origin in the mystery cults of Asia, and when it confronted the Hellenistic culture of the early Christian centuries, it was certainly influenced by the underlying motifs of that fermenting cultural milieu. The central motif of the age was the quest for salvation, which was to be brought into our world by a transcendent being. Men of the late Roman Empire were world-weary, yearning for deliverance of the soul from the crushing burden of the body and the world in which it was imprisoned. The body and the world were material, evil, transient, and confining. The need was to escape into a spiritual world—good, permanent, and liberating. This general religion of the time Hans Jonas calls "a dualistic, transcendent religion of salvation."[38]

Gnosticism came into this milieu, emphasizing *gnōsis*—not rational knowledge of dogmas, but a secret, revealed knowledge of God, the soul, and the world. It was a suprarational knowledge, supernaturally *revealed*. The revelation itself took place not in simple instruction, but in a solemn cultic act. The revelation was an act of encounter, not the passing on of knowledge. It was a saving encounter, for the knowledge acquired is mystical, uniting the knower and the known. The knower is transformed by the knowledge, because it is a new relation and gives a new identity to the knower. The knowledge is not there to be shaped into dogma and transmitted to others as propositional truth. Others too must acquire the knowledge through the mystical encounter.

Now, it was not in this form that Irenaeus encountered the gnosticism of Valentinus and Basilides, Cerinthus and Marcion. Gnosticism itself had been hellenized into a system of speculative dogmas. At least that is the form in which he has written about it. These Christian gnostics, who had made a new product out of elements from Hellenism, Christianity, and Oriental mystery religions, claimed the authority of a secret tradition stemming from the apostles for what they taught. Gnosticism, in its hellenized, pseudointellectual form, was thus an internal problem of the Christian church.

As opposed to the Gnostic claims about what the apostles taught, Irenaeus and Hippolytus had to produce different sets of propositions as the real body of knowledge handed down by the apostles. One cannot say that this was a clear case of pseudomorphosis. For Irenaeus, being an Asian himself, was fully aware that the truth could not be reduced to propositional formulae. But he had sown the seed for a doctrine of authority that was later to work havoc in the life of the church, namely, that the truth is to be formulated out of the Scriptures and by the magisterium of the church.

In Origen, that prolific genius of Alexandria, we find this pseudomorphosis further advanced:

> Just as there are many among Greeks and barbarians alike [probably a reference to the various schools of Gnostics] who promise us the truth, and yet we gave up seeking for it from all who claimed it for false opinions after we had become convinced that we must learn the truth from him: in the same way when we find many who think they hold the doctrine of Christ, some of them differing in their beliefs from the Christians of earlier times, and yet the teaching of the Church, handed down in unbroken succession from the Apostles, is still preserved and continues to exist in the churches up to the present day, we maintain that *that only is to be believed as the truth which in no way conflicts with the tradition of the church and the Apostles.*
>
> But the following fact should be understood: The holy Apostles, when preaching the faith of Christ (*fidem Christi*), *took certain doctrines*, those namely

which they believed to be necessary ones, and deliv-
ered them in the plainest terms to all believers, even
to such as appeared to be somewhat dull in the investigation of divine knowledge. The grounds of their
statements they left to be investigated by such as
should merit the higher gifts of the spirit, and in particular by such as should afterwards receive through
the holy Spirit Himself the graces of language, wisdom
and knowledge. There were other doctrines, however,
about which the Apostles simply said that things were
so, keeping silence as to the how or why; their intention undoubtedly being to supply the more diligent of
those who came after them, such as should prove to be
lovers of wisdom, with an exercise on which to display
the fruit of their ability.[39]

The Christian faith appears here to have been reduced to a
set of formulated doctrines, with a few unclarified doctrines
left behind by the apostles in order that later theologians may
have something to chew on.

KNOWLEDGE AND ETHICS

Equally superficial is Origen's understanding of the relation
between doctrine and ethics. Ethics is a consequence of a
doctrine, namely, "the doctrine of the righteous judgment of
God, a doctrine which, if believed to be pure, summons its
hearers to live a good life and by every means to avoid sin."

This encyclopedic mind of ancient Christianity shows no
depth of perception in the understanding of human free will
either. The main difference between living beings and inanimate beings lies in this: Living beings cause motion from
within; inanimate objects have to be moved from without.
Movement from within living beings is caused by images in
consciousness creating an impulse. Rational animals are different from the *alogoi* ("beasts"), in that the former can judge
between the various images and therefore be selective in their
effective impulses. It is the free will which chooses which

impulse to follow. Education is the capacity to regulate one's impulses and to discern in dispassionate wisdom which impulses are good and which bad.

Thus man's freedom consists in the capacity to regulate one's impulses. Origen here stands in the great tradition of Hellenism which exalts both reason and freedom, making them inseparable, though reason always precedes the ethical will.

Origen thus escapes at least in part from the intellectualist pseudomorphosis of Christianity by positing a fairly high role for human freedom, albeit limited by the providence of God. Free will is never alone in acting, but without human freedom certain actions cannot be explained. Planting the crops and watering them are works of free will. However, it is not free will, but God that gives the increase.

> It is, then, neither in our power to make progress apart from the knowledge of God, nor does the knowledge of God compel us to do so, unless we ourselves contribute something towards the good result.[40]

The Cappadocian Fathers

Origen developed also what was later to become a disastrous weapon in the hands of the Arians, the method of using proof texts to demonstrate the truthfulness of doctrines. Christ and the apostles had used texts from the Old Testment—but that was mainly to establish the identity of Jesus as the Messiah foretold by the prophets, not to prove doctrines. Doctrinal speculation of this kind had its precedents in the Apologists of an earlier era. But they never had the influence in the church which Origen's writings had.

When we come to the Cappadocian fathers (Basil, Gregory Nazianzen, and Gregory of Nyssa), we find the right synthesis between the Biblical realism of Antioch and the speculative genius of Alexandria. Cappadocian theology is a magnificent blend of the gospel with elements of Hellenic philosophy, Oriental mysticism (direct awareness of God's majesty, love, and holiness), Antiochian realism, and Alexandrian theoretical speculation. It still amazes us by its rich contemporaneity.

On the matter of the relation between knowledge and ethical action, it is Gregory Nazianzen who makes the position clear. His fundamental affirmation is that knowledge of God is dependent on ethical maturity. He who does right alone can know the truth. Unlike Origen, Nazianzen affirms the primacy of the ethical:

> Not to everyone, my friends, does it belong to philosophize about God; not to every one—the subject is not so cheap and low—and I will add not to every audience, not at all times, not on all points; but on certain occasions, and before certain persons, and within certain limits . . . . It is when we are free from all defilement or disturbance, and when that which rules within us is not confused with vexatious or erring images.[41]

This is a basically Biblical insight. Paul says the same in his prayer for the Colossians (ch. 1:10), that they may "lead a life worthy of the Lord, fully pleasing to him, bearing fruit in every good work and increasing in the knowledge of God." Growth in the cognitive is correlated to growth in the ethical. To put it differently, the creatively ethical (bearing fruit in every good work) is an aspect of the knowledge of God.

Here is an important answer to the questions: How do I know God? How do I live my life? The two questions are inseparable, and the answers to both have to be sought simultaneously. Sound Christian teaching has to keep the two together. This is what the pastoral epistles[42] call "sound teaching" (*hugiainousa didaskalia*). It is healthy and health-giving teaching that helps man grow to the fullness of his stature. Faith itself grows only by "works." A guilty conscience leads to the shipwreck of faith, as the letter to Timothy says (II Tim. 2:19).

It is only in our doing that our knowing is clarified, con-

firmed and augmented. Basil says in his letter to Maximus the
philosopher:

> We are delighted to find you not slothful in your
> attitude towards the first and greatest of virtues—love
> towards both God and neighbour. We hold as an indi-
> cation of the latter your tenderness for me; as a proof
> of the former, your enthusiasm for knowledge. That
> everything is contained in these two is known to every
> disciple of Christ.[43]

Pseudomorphosis sets in when the knowledge of God is separated from the love and worship of God and from the love
and service of fellowmen.

For the Cappadocians, however, the ethical could not be
separated from the cultic. The two together constituted holiness, which was the true matrix of the knowledge of God.
Holiness is not merely a matter of ethical purity. It involves
transfiguration of the very being of man into the likeness and
image of God. It is in worship that man becomes transfigured
and therefore enabled both to be ethically good and thus to
know God.

By worship is meant, however, much more than being
gathered together to hear the word of God. That is only one
aspect, the preliminary stage, of the worship of God, open to
Christians and non-Christians alike. True worship is access
into the presence of God, which follows the hearing of the
Word, and is open only to the baptized.

The Eucharist is not merely a means of grace, or a *verbum
visibile*, as Augustine taught. It is the supreme and central act
of the church, which is the authentic milieu for the knowledge
of God. Here the veil between God and man is torn in the
broken body of Christ, and we lift up our hearts to where
Christ stands at the right hand of the Father.

How do we know God? In this act of the community, where
the veil is drawn aside, where the community, united with
Christ and with each other by the spirit, gives itself in Christ
to the Father, and the Father gives himself to us in Christ.

That is relevation—an event, not a body of knowledge, not a book. Revelation is face-to-face encounter with God in love, calling him Abba, Father. And it takes place supremely in this act of the Eucharistic offering and communion. And true knowledge of God can take place only in the encounter, not in theology.

The revelation of God is not an act which closed either with the ascension or with the death of the last apostle. It is not an event of the past recorded in the Bible, which we then study by analytical-critical examination of the texts. The unveiling that took place in Christ continues to this day in the encounter of the Eucharist. The Bible has its honored place in that encounter. Theology can hold the torch to that encounter. But neither of these, nor even the personal encounter of pietism and fundamentalism, can take the place of the rendezvous which Christ himself established, when he said, "Do this in remembrance of me."

The Cappadocians and the Knowledge of God

The Cappadocian fathers make four fundamental assertions that seem to be of the greatest possible importance for the facing of the current crisis of authority in the church.

1. Worship and ethics, the love of God and the love of man together constitute the only milieu in which there can be a true knowledge of God and therefore authentic theology. Theology cannot be spun out in the professor's study. It has to come out of the life of worship of the church and out of the life of Christians in the world. Basil is explicit on this point.

> I repeat, knowledge is manifold—it involves perception of our creator, recognition of His wonderful works, observance of His commandments and intimate communion with Him. . . . Thou shalt put them, it is said, before the testimony, and I shall be known of thee thence. . . . The statement that God shall be known from the mercy-seat means that He will be

known to His worshippers. And "the Lord knoweth them that are His," means that on account of their good works He receives them into intimate communion with Him.

Or again:

If it [the mind] has yielded to the aid of the spirit, it will have understanding of the truth, and will know God. But it will know Him, as the Apostle says, in part; and in the life to come more perfectly. . . . We say that we know our God from his operations, but do not undertake to approach near to His essence.

The current crisis of authority can be overcome, not by a new theology, but by the self-authenticating quality of life centered in quickened Eucharistic worship and selfless service to fellowmen in the context of current issues. It is a difficult balance to maintain in our contemporary world. And yet where it is practiced, a quality of authenticity enters the picture and draws men to it. A striking example of this kind of spirituality is the Protestant monastic community of Taizé in France, or the Catholic communities of the Little Brothers and Little Sisters of Jesus. Here we see the alienation of theology from worship and ethics being gradually overcome.

2. The Cappadocian fathers insist also that God in his essence is basically incomprehensible, and to pretend to have conceptual knowledge of him is dishonest. Here Nazianzen flings a taunt even at Plato for having pretended to have known God:

To conceive God is difficult, to express him in words is impossible, says a Greek teacher of divinity[44] quite cleverly, I think, with the intention that he might be thought to have apprehended him, since he says it is difficult, but he can evade the responsibility of giving expression to the conception, since that is admitted to be impossible. But according to me, to express him in words is impossible, to conceive him mentally is even more impossible.[45]

Gregory insists that God has not made himself incomprehensible out of jealousy. Incomprehensibility belongs to his very essence as pure, undetermined, free being.

> What God is in nature (*phusis*) and essence (*ousia*),
> no man has ever yet discovered, or can discover.
> Whether it will ever be discovered is a question which
> he who will may examine and decide.[46]

He thinks that such knowledge is possible only in ultimate union with God.

And yet we Christians are guilty of having falsely claimed to know about God and to be able to teach our knowledge of God to all and sundry. We need to come back to a confession of our ignorance, for the sake of honesty as well as to reduce the credibility gap between Christians and non-Christians. This will also preclude the cheap evangelization of adherents to other faiths with our superior knowledge of God—so arrogant and so repelling.

3. The Cappadocians insist that God cannot be located in time or space, inside or outside this universe. It would be a great insult to the intelligence of our fourth-century fathers to accuse them of having believed in a God "up there" or "out there." Gregory Nazianzen, after having established by strict logic that God is not a body, goes on to ask:

> Is He nowhere or somewhere? If He is nowhere [i.e.,
> not in space] then some questioning soul may demand
> —how can He then be said to exist? For if the non-
> existent is nowhere, then that which is nowhere may
> perhaps also be non-existent. But if He is somewhere,
> He must be either in the universe or beyond the uni-
> verse. If *in* the universe, He must be either in a part
> or in the whole. If in some part, then He is circum-
> scribed by the part which is less than Himself; but if
> He is in the whole universe, then He is circumscribed
> by that which is greater than the universe, namely that
> which circumscribes universe. For the universe is
> place, and no place is free from circumscription.[47]

If, after having read these words written in the fourth century, we assume our fathers to have believed in a three-storey universe, with God dwelling on the upper floor, that reveals little more than our own naïveté and sad parochialism.

4. Despite his unlocatability and incomprehensibility, he can be known by us, not in his *ousia*, but in terms of his *energia* or operations in our world. One has to purify oneself by worship and obedience in order to gain this knowledge. Basil makes this clear in his letters 234 and 235. Gregory of Nyssa has this to say in the Great Catechism:

> And so one who rigorously explores the depths of the mystery receives in his spirit a mysterious and moderate apprehension of the teaching of God's nature. But he is unable to explain with logical clarity the ineffable depth of this mystery. For example, how can the same thing (i.e., the Trinity) be capable of being numbered, and yet reject numeration? How can it be observed with distinctions and yet be apprehended as a monad? How can it be distinct in personality yet same in substance? . . . For it is as if the number of triad were a remedy in the case of those in error as to the one (the Jews) and the assertion of unity for those whose beliefs are dispersed among a number of divinities.[48]

CHAPTER IV
Free God
and Free Man

Gregory of Nyssa, father of the universal church, has been neglected by Western students and almost rejected on various false charges—Platonism, Origenism, and Semi-Pelagianism. The recovery of this father and his teaching seems to be the *sine qua non* for Western theology, whether Catholic or Protestant, to regain its equilibrium and its sense of direction. He is more than merely an antidote to many of the Augustinian distortions in Western theology. He can give us the groundwork for a theology that does justice to contemporary humanism and our interest in science and technology.

No doubt there is much of Plato and Origen in him. Pelagius probably read Gregory, but if our reconstruction of Pelagius' arguments is correct, he did not understand the depths of Gregory. As for Platonism and Origenism, Gregory has filtered them through the authentic tradition of the church, and gives to us the only kind of theology there is—the Christian tradition interpreted and enriched through the categories and concepts of the philosophers and church fathers with a few creative contributions here and there.

Two excellent studies have been made of Gregory's thought by French-speaking scholars. They seem to be capable of greater penetration into Eastern thought than their Anglo-

Saxon colleagues, although this is not to overlook the value of Gregorian studies by Werner Jaeger[49] and Hans von Balthasar.[50] The studies by Jerome Gaith and Roger Leys, which appeared about the same time as Jaeger's great work, could not fully take into account the fruits of Jaeger's more definitive edition. Yet they provide in a brief compass, and in relation to two of Gregory's key concepts, an overview of his thought. Gaith's *La Conception de la liberté chez Grégoire de Nysse* was published in Paris in 1953 in the series *Études de philosophie médiévale*, edited by Étienne Gilson. Leys' *L'Image de Dieu chez Saint Grégoire de Nysse* was published in 1951 (Paris: Desclée de Brouwer).

AUGUSTINE AND NYSSA

Apart from Augustine, Gregory of Nyssa was among the boldest of Christian thinkers. Augustine worked with the categories of human sinfulness and divine sovereignty, and therefore emphasized the huge *gap* between God and man. Nyssa on the contrary saw the freedom of man as the central element to which everything was to be related, and therefore looked for the same freedom in the very essence of God, and so sought for *common ground* between God and man.

In the Augustinian West, God and man are essentially heteronatural. In the Gregorian East, God and man are essentially connatural. The two emphases both have their place in the authentic tradition. But Western theology is too one-sided in its traditional emphasis on God's sovereignty and on man's submissiveness. These concepts of the West are also to be found in the more inclusive Eastern tradition, but they are adequately balanced by the notions of the freedom and kingship of man.

In a Greek society fettered by its notion of *heimarmenē* ("fate"), Gregory's emphasis on freedom as the basis of human virtue was not without its Hellenic antecedents. But by positing freedom in God, man, and the universe, Gregory has forged for us a fresh way to come to terms with reality that seems particularly appropriate to our time.

Augustine saw only the depraved state of fallen man and created a pessimistic anthropology out of that. Gregory saw the tension between man as he now appears (disintegrating and desperate) and what he really is by virtue of his creation. Mankind dreams constantly of becoming something else than what it now is. This nostalgia for home points to his true nature. He is now in bondage to something which is not his real nature. Freedom means attainment to the dynamic and true nature of man.

Gregory's writings are addressed to two different types of readers—to the literate masses and the philosophically trained elite. In the latter class come definitely two of his brief but difficult works—On the Soul and the Resurrection and On the Making of Man. Equally philosophical, though somewhat longer, is his Life of Moses. It is in these three works that Gregory reveals his more original and bold thinking. He seems to be afraid of offending the common people by placing such dangerous ideas before them. But even in his boldness he is aware of the limitations of human thought, the incapacity of the mind of man to penetrate the mysteries of the universe. He therefore often fails to develop some of his ideas systematically. So much the better for us, for that may be the reason why they still sound so fresh and contemporary.

What is even more problematic is that much of what Gregory teaches goes against the grain of what is regarded as authoritative Christian teaching in the West. On the question of original sin, for example, it is difficult to reconcile Nyssa's ideas with those of Augustine. But the latter have unfortunately become authoritative for the West.

Nyssa has to be seen and read with fresh vision—not within the categories of Western theology. The grandeur and misery of man, his royal destiny and his pining away in bondage, the presence of evil and the fact of change, the need for alienated man to become true Man—these are the themes of his choice.

The Freedom of God and the Freedom of Man

There is no way of coming to terms with the freedom of man except by treating it in relation to the freedom of God himself. To presuppose a measure of conflict between God's grace and man's freedom, or between God's sovereignty or predestination and man's freedom, seems to be the basic error of Western theology.

If man is created in the image of God, argues Nyssa, then he should have all the good things in the prototype, and among these the most important, freedom from necessity, independence, and sovereignty (autonomy).[51] If man is created in the image of God, then either God must be mortal and sinful as we are, or else we have to become immortal, free and holy as he is. There is no other alternative. And therefore the negation of the liberty of man is the negation of the freedom of God. If man does not become free, God would be bound. The liberation of man thus takes on an urgency and the character of an imperative.

Is God free? The freedom of God is studied by Nyssa in terms of his transcendence and his immanence. The Stoic regarded God as totally immanent. For Aristotle the Pure Act is totally transcendent. The unmoved Mover of Aristotle's metaphysics has no relation to this world, for it neither creates the world nor knows it. It moves the world by the world's attraction toward it (*eros*). The same is basically true of Plato and Plotinus. But for Plotinus at least the universe is an emanation from the One who remains immobile, as the light comes from the sun, "who does not move." As the fire generates heat, so the One has generated the universe.

Gregory has obviously learned from all of them, but when he sets forth his doctrine of God, it is something more than a mere synthesis:

> God, being the Unique Good, in a simple non-composite nature, ever beholds himself, and never subjects

himself to change according to the impulsions of his
will, but eternally wills that which he is and is always
that which he wills.[52]

All of it can be traced back in bits and pieces to Neo-
platonic writers. Hellenistic metaphysics lies behind this conception of God. But what is important here for Gregory is
God's independence of the universe. Unlike the Stoic God,
who as the soul of the universe cannot exist apart from the
cosmos, Gregory's God is totally transcendent, totally free of
the created order.

But then where did the material universe come from? Is it
outside God or in God? Either it is outside God, in which
case it is coeternal with God, or it is in God, in which case
God himself is material, for how can the immaterial contain
the material?

That is really a tough question. And Gregory's answer is
more comprehensible to twentieth-century man with his advanced knowledge of physics, but it must have been quite
difficult for his contemporaries. It is a simple answer: Matter
itself is spiritual, or as we would say today, matter is a mode
of energy.

And what is the source of this energy, which now appears
as matter? Gregory wrote at a time when Julian the Apostate
had reinstated polytheism in the Empire, and when Manichaeism with its (negative) affirmation of matter as eternal
and as the source of evil was having its heyday in Asia Minor.
Both polytheism and Manichaeism are affronts to the freedom
of God, for they present powers opposed to God, over whom
he has no control.

EVIL AND FREEDOM

The existence of evil was the fact from which Manichaeism
took its start. To explain the presence of evil in the world
and in man was a challenge to any sensitive and inquiring
mind. Augustine was forced to acknowledge the presence of

freedom in the creation, simply because he too had to explain the origin of evil. But he conceded freedom reluctantly. When his own anti-Manichaean writings about freedom were used against him by the Pelagians, he had to underplay freedom even further.

Gregory disposes of the problem of the existence of evil as an affront to the freedom of God by a very dramatic and courageous intellectual step which Augustine found very helpful in his own thought. Gregory's answer to the problem of evil is developed in three steps:

1. Physical evil cannot really be regarded as evil.
2. Moral evil has no ultimate reality.
3. Moral evil is to be explained as the absence of good.

By physical evil, Gregory means the inequalities among men for which they are not responsible. But those, he suggests, insofar as they are not the consequence of an evil will, cannot be regarded as evil. Moral evil, on the other hand, has its own reality—as sin, vice, injustice. But these are actually the absence of righteousness, virtue, justice. They are privations in being (state of sin) or refusals to be (sinful acts). It is a negation of the true being of man. The being of man is created, but not its negation. Only that which is created exists, for creation is the will of God, as we shall see below. That which is the negation of creation is therefore ontologically nonexistent. "That which is not, has no reality, and that which has no reality is not the work of the one who has created reality." [53]

But moral evil is a moral reality, insists Gregory. It is an act of a will that is free. "The will of an evil God," say the Manichaeans. But if this God is capable only of evil, he is not free. If all his acts are evil, i.e., privation of good, then he himself represents the privation of being. And if he is not free, then he is not God. Moral evil can come only from the created being, free and capable of both good and evil.

This drama of evil is not a mere hallucination. It is the

arena of the true liberation of man. But of that, more later. The point here is that God's freedom is not limited by the presence of evil. Gregory's perception of the nature of evil offers much to a modern mind dissatisfied with Augustine's categorical denial of any good in man and with the vision of man as totally evil.

It is unfair to accuse Gregory of some form of Semi-Pelagianism, since Pelagius himself got his basic ideas only through a misunderstanding of Gregory. Gregory does not deny the fact that man is sinful or evil. But he would categorically reject the allegation that human nature is evil. After all, nature is that which is given to a being by its creator, that which constitutes his true and fully developed being. Gregory would say not only that human nature is good, but also that it is the *perfection* of all good, and also that that good has to be a free good in order to be perfect.

In other words, if we use the word "nature" in its strict sense, nature is that which a newborn being is destined to be. The acorn of the oak has the oak tree as its nature, something that the seed could become, given the necessary combination of soil, water, air, etc., even though it may fail to reach its destiny. So also human nature is man's destiny to become a full human being. And for a full human being the decisive factor is that he is to be in the image of God. The nature of man is thus the image of God—not sin or evil. Pelagius never grasped this philosophical aspect of Gregory's thinking, and so argued with Augustine on a purely ethical basis. The thinking of Pelagius and the thinking of Gregory do not belong to the same level, and it is thus unfair to understand Gregory in Pelagian terms.

Evil is of course there, the consequence of the decisions and actions of a created being, free to choose between good and evil. It is primordial in creation, but not eternal. Evil is prior to man, and has come to man from the outside. It does not belong to his nature, for nature is what man was created with, and that creation, being an act of God, cannot be evil.

Evil, which is external to the true nature of man, has come to him from outside as Paul says (Rom., ch. 5). Human freedom opened the door to evil, and evil became lodged within human existence. Evil cannot be eradicated without the assistance of the grace of God. Sin has gained mastery over man and man has become a slave of evil, unable to liberate himself.

However, liberation from this enslavement to evil can be only part of the total development of man. The salvation of man is not to be understood merely in a negative sense, as deliverance from sin and death. Sin (moral evil) and death (loss of being resulting from moral evil) are enemies to be vanquished. Man must become capable of doing good (the opposite of sin) and should possess being that is not subject to death. But these are both negative ways of understanding salvation. Gregory would say that evil is an element in the arena of human existence that can enhance human freedom. True freedom comes, however, not merely in the negative struggle against evil, but in the heroic and worshipful process of striving to create the good in every situation. The fact that evil is there not only as the enemy of the good we would create, but also falsely taking on the form of a good (pleasure, comfort, security, glory, honor, power, etc.), ensures that our choice of the good is a genuine act of freedom, i.e., that the good is chosen in a strenuous mood and despite the difficulties, rather than by an easy habit in which no decision or choice is required.

Evil can thus help the growth of true humanity in freedom, by its very presence demanding from man difficult and strenuous choices between evil and good in situations where it is much easier to choose the evil. It is in the struggle against evil that man develops true freedom—against evil within one's own self as well as in the structures of society and in other persons and situations.

But evil cannot be ultimate, for then evil would be eternal. Evil exists as the manifestation of being which refuses to become what its destiny indicates, and thereby inevitably moves toward nonbeing. Evil is being-toward-death, and ultimately, when death itself is removed, then evil will also have been removed, for death is the consequence of evil.

THE INCOMPREHENSIBILITY OF GOD AS AN ASPECT OF HIS TRANSCENDENCE

For Plotinus as for Origen, who follows the same line, the incomprehensibility of God is an accident of our mind, due to its being locked up in a material body. But the original contribution of Gregory of Nyssa lies in the fact that he makes this incomprehensibility an essential element of God's transcendence. Whoever "Dionysius the Areopagite" may have been, he too agrees with Nyssa against Plotinus in his understanding of divine incomprehensibility as belonging to God's essence. Nazianzen would say that his incomprehensibility (which is also his transcendence) is the only thing we can know of God's essence.

The failure to grasp this truth adequately is at the root of all the errors of Origen, which led to so many diverse heresies, including Arianism and Sabellianism. For Origen, as for Plotinus, God was simple, One, Spirit, the source and origin of all intellectual and spiritual nature.[54] He thought he knew God, as Plato thought he did. The Cappadocians and Pseudo-Dionysius insist, on the other hand, that no concept, no created intelligence, can comprehend God.

In fact, Basil would insist that not only God, but even created beings, cannot be comprehended in their essence, the *Ding an sich*. It is only the properties of the object that we can conceptually grasp. Their essence remains beyond knowledge. This would hardly be acceptable to Husserlian phenomenology. But the Cappadocians regard the awareness of the final incomprehensibility of God and his creation as itself a gift of grace, an experience of deep and foundation-shaking reality.

In Nyssa's Life of Moses we are told that the higher we go up Mt. Zion toward the presence of God, the clearer becomes the absolute incomprehensibility of the divine nature. But that spiritual ascent is itself a rich experience which remains conceptually ineffable. Without that deep and disturbing awareness of the incomprehensibility of God, too many of us have dared into the realm of theology, making statements about God at random, without restraint. We theologians created a God in our own image, or in the image of our glorious Caesars and Napoleons, and it is this God who has recently died. *Requiescat in pace!*

Granting that human intelligence cannot comprehend God, one might yet ask, *Do we not know God by faith?* Gregory's answer to this question would be: If you mean knowing the essence of God, no. For God dwells in light unapproachable, beyond the abyss of darkness, where even faith cannot penetrate in knowledge. Faith helps only to see the mysterious and hidden inaccessibility of God's essence and yet to trust in him who reveals his presence but not his essence. It is not just space and time that hide us from him; they are but symbols of an inner alienation of man from his constitutive reality. By faith the alienation is broken, but God remains incomprehensible.

THE FREEDOM OF IMMANENCE

God's immanence, according to Gregory, does not contradict his freedom. Here is another of his truly original contributions. But in order to grasp his notion of free immanence in the creation, we have to come to terms with his very notion of creation.

As has been said earlier, the creation is not an emanation from the essence of God. It is not an extension of his being, but a product of his will. It is this will which constitutes the principles (*aformas*), the causes (*aitias*), and the energies (*dunameis*) of all created things. Matter and its various forms

are thus, so to speak, the concretions of the divine will. It is
God's will that is the very being of creation. And God is
immanent in creation by will, not by *ousia*, or essence. But
because it is the dynamic will of God who is freedom, the
creation itself is dynamic and free.

In the fourth century Gregory already was an out-and-out
evolutionist in his doctrine of creation. In his dialogue On
the Soul and the Resurrection, he puts the following words
into his sister's mouth:

> Scripture informs us that the Deity proceeded by a
> sort of graduated and ordered advance to the creation
> of man. After the foundations of the universe were
> laid, as the history records, man did not appear on
> the earth at once, but the creation of the brutes pre-
> ceded his, and the plants preceded them. Thereby
> Scripture shows that the forces of life blended with
> bodily nature according to a gradation, first it infused
> itself into insensate nature, and in continuation of this
> advanced into the sentient world, and then ascended
> to intelligent and rational beings.[55]

The world is good. Gregory has no doubt about it.

> This will [God's] that has in its power to do all
> things will have no tendency to anything that is evil
> (for impulse towards evil is foreign to God's nature)
> but . . . whatever is good, this it also wishes, and
> wishing, is able to perform, and being able, will not
> fail to perform, but . . . it will bring all its proposals
> for good to effectual accomplishment. Now the world
> is good, and all its contents are seen to be wisely and
> skillfully ordered.[56]

The "how" of creation Gregory recognized to be perennially
problematic—in fact, beyond the reach of the human intellect.
Says Macrina:

> Reason cannot see *how* the visible comes out of the
> invisible, how the hard solid comes out of the in-
> tangible, how the finite comes out of the infinite, how

that which is circumscribed by certain propositions, where the idea of quantity comes in, can come from that which has no size and so on.[57]

Or earlier:

In order, then, to avoid falling into . . . these absurdities, which the enquiry into the origin of things involves, let us, following the example of the Apostle, leave the question of *how* in each created being, without meddling with it at all, but merely observing incidentally that the motion of God's will becomes at the moment of His choice a reality, and the intention becomes at once realized as a nature.[58]

God's immanence in creation should thus not be misunderstood as the presence of his *ousia* in the cosmos. It is because the very *ousia* of the cosmos is the will of God that we speak of immanence at all. This immanence by will does not imprison God in creation. He remains free.

But his will is a dynamic will. It is constantly in motion toward a goal, a purpose. Why this purpose is also not immediately achieved is also a matter of God's choice. He has willed it so. Despite the fall and the consequent coarsening of material existence, the material creation is still moved by the will of God toward its God-appointed destiny. Human history itself, says Gregory, is in movement toward a point, when the succession of birth and death shall cease, and humanity will be reconstituted in the resurrection. To this we shall revert later, when dealing with God's immanence in man.

Man, the Image of God

Gregory insists that the "chief end of man" is more than merely beholding God and enjoying him: "God has made us not simply spectators of the power of God, but also participants in his very nature." [59]

This *koinōnia* with God, this belonging by our very structure to the nature of God, sounds blasphemous to many Western thinkers. And yet this is the soul of the Eastern tradition. "God became man that man may become God." If not by creation, at least by the incarnation we have been made participants in God's nature (*theias koinōnoi phuseōs,* II Peter 1:4). Not because, as in Plotinus, the soul is an emanation from God, but rather because God has in his freedom chosen to impart this grace to man.

For it is in order to manifest himself that God has made man. God did not make man because he needed to do it. Rather, in his superabundant love and freedom, he chose to create a being like himself, in whom he would reveal himself. Gregory insists that this very creation was an act of free grace. The incarnation completes it. But the incarnation itself is possible because in the very creation there is a connaturality and even proportionality (a quantitative term which should normally not be used in this connection) between God and man.

This, of course, would be unbearable to those brought up in the early Barthian tradition. A choice has to be made between early Barth or Basil and Gregory of Nyssa.

There is here no identification, *à la Shankara,* between God and man. God remains free and transcendent. Man is part of the creation, but to be distinguished from the rest of creation by the fact that he alone is created in the image of God. God is immanent in man in a manner different from that in which he is immanent by will in the creation. For man was not created in exactly the same way as the rest of creation. God said, "Let there be light" and there was light. In the case of man, it was not the *word* of God, but the deliberative counsel of God ("Let us make man in our image") and consequently the *hand* of God which molded him, and the *breath* (spirit) of God which was breathed into his nostrils. It is still a free immanence of the transcendent God which does not bind God. Yet it is a special kind of immanence. Man is aware of this presence within him, though enfeebled by the environment in which he has come to be. But there is in man, *pace* Barth, an inborn knowledge of God, a deep desire to behold him, and even to become like him, which is his true vocation. Man need not, however, go entirely out of himself, to know God, for God is also "the beyond in our midst," at the depths of our very being. "He who has purified his [inner] eye, he who has purified his heart, sees in the beauty of his own self the image of the divine nature." [60]

Jerome Gaith has drawn our attention to the fact that for Gregory the prefix *meta* (as in "metaphysical") always has two meanings—both "beyond" and "in the interior," "above" and "in the depths"—for it denotes both the transcendent and the immanent aspects of God.[61]

But this immanence of God in the soul of man is not a static fact. It increases and decreases in the measure in which the soul opens itself up to and approaches the transcendent freedom of God.

God and Man

Gregory does not take the transcendence of man too lightly. The following passage demonstrates how realistic he is about the intellectual capacities of man, even in the pre-Kantian fourth century.

> The creation can never, by its intellectual efforts, get out of itself, but it remains enclosed in itself. Whatever it sees, it is itself that it sees—even when it imagines that it has attained to some transcendent object. It constantly seeks to go beyond itself, in its knowledge of being, to jump beyond the gap (*diastēma*) but it never really succeeds. For in each object that it discovers with the mind it discerns always also this inherent gap [distension] in the understanding of its nature, this gap [distension] is nothing but the creation itself.[62]

But this excellent good which we have learned to seek and to cherish, being beyond the created order, is also beyond the intellect. For how can our understanding, travelling across the multiplicity caused by the distension of creation, be able to grasp the undistended nature through temporal analysis by which it always seeks to grasp the antecedents of all it finds? Of course, it can by its incessant activity go beyond all the objects of its knowledge, but to lift itself beyond the very category of time is beyond its means, for it cannot take its stance outside of itself, nor can it escape its set limits or even time itself.

The human intellect, at this point, is somewhat like a man who finds himself at the extreme point of a jutting promontory. Let us imagine a deep red rock, slippery and precipitous. It is a mountain of immense height and at the summit, there is this narrow jutting promontory standing over a vast abyss. What would be the experience of a man who advances along the edge of this slippery rock, and suddenly finds no place to set his foot or get a hold for his hand? That would be the experience of a soul, who in intellectual pursuit of the non-temporal and the non-spatial, leaves the *terra firma* of finite things. Having neither place, nor time, nor measure, nor anything of that kind to hold on to, reason seeks to grasp the ungraspable and is seized by dizziness (*hilligia*). Not knowing where to turn next, reason comes back to that which is familiar, and is happy to believe simply that the Transcendent is other than all that it knows.

That is why, when the discussion gets beyond what can be discussed, it is time to stop . . . and to follow the example of the great souls who have spoken about God himself. "Who shall speak of the marvels of the Lord?" and "I shall speak of thy *works!*" . . . "This generation shall praise thy *works*." So in the discourse about God, when the enquiry turns to the divine essence, it is time to stop; if on the contrary it takes for its object some beneficent energy of which the knowledge comes down to us, then we can praise its power, recount its miracles, describe its works, and thus make use of the discourse.[63]

Gregory should not therefore be accused of taking God too lightly by proposing connaturality between God and man. The actual finitude of man is by no means overlooked.

All that we can know of God is what he does, his energies, his action. There is some point therefore in contemporary theology focusing on the acts of God and on the God who acts. That emphasis does not come merely from the activist tempo of our age. It has genuine patristic roots. But to claim that in Jesus Christ God has completely revealed himself and therefore to conceive of God in terms of the incarnate Jesus Christ, may at best be unwise, at worst blasphemous. It is one who has known Jesus Christ who says to us:

> One does not know God except in terms of our incapacity to apprehend him.[64]

Christian claims to have a special channel or source of knowledge of God, whether it be in the historical Jesus or in the Scriptures, should therefore be quite suspect. God's transcendence and freedom remain, even after the incarnation. The incomprehensibility of God has not been done away with in Jesus Christ. Only the Christian who has experienced both the vertigo consequent on trying to know God conceptually and the awareness of our incapacity to do so can truly worship the free, transcendent God.

THE KNOWLEDGE OF THE TRANSCENDENT

If God is so utterly and radically transcendent, then what knowledge of God is possible?

> Blessed are the pure in heart,
> for they shall see God.

The sixth discourse on the Beatitudes is the *locus classicus* of Gregory's understanding of the knowledge of God. What is available to us is the knowledge of man, and through the image in ourselves, we can see a reflection of the glory of God. That is why no knowledge of God is possible until the image is made pure. By making man what he ought to be, we can begin to see who God is. When man becomes "pure in heart," i.e., devoid of all evil, then he begins to see God. Only holiness (sanctity), not theology, can lead to the knowledge of God.

THE INCARNATION

And that is the point of the incarnation, the church, and the "sacraments." Jesus Christ is born, that he may die. He lived before he was "born," so he could not have been born in order to live. The death of Jesus was not the consequence of his birth; the birth was accepted in order that he might die and through dying overcome death in man. The body in which he was born was taken out of the same lump as our bodies, and in the resurrection of his body our bodies too shall participate.[65]

But he is the pure image too. In Jesus Christ the God-man the identity of God the prototype and man the image become merged. In Jesus Christ the image was an undistorted mirror of the archetype.

By faith and baptism we ourselves are united to this original image, and we become partners in his resurrection life. The Eucharist is the continuing participation in this resurrection life.[66] The Eucharist as the body of Christ gradually transmutes us into itself. This continual deification, as it advances in self-discipline, prayer, and acts of love toward fellowmen, makes us also transparent to Deity. That alone is the true knowledge of God.

> For that change in our life which takes place through regeneration will not be change, if we continue in that state in which we were. . . . For what you have not become, that you are not. "As many as received him,"

thus speaks the Gospel of those who have been born again, "to them gave he power to become the sons of God." . . . If, then, you have received God, if you have become a child of God, make manifest in your disposition the God that is in you, manifest in yourself Him that begot you.[67]

Holiness of life comes when God begins to manifest himself in us. And in such manifestation through the image, according to Nyssa, we know God.

THE UNITY OF MAN IN THE IMAGE OF GOD

The aspect of Nyssa's thought which we have just discussed should sound so strange in modern Western ears that it would take a total spiritual reconditioning even to listen to it adequately. There are other aspects of the image of God and the freedom of man in Nyssa's thought, however, which should be readily acceptable even to many secular minds.

To do justice to Gregory's thought, one has to begin with what may appear as farfetched and even weird—his conception of the two creations of man, and in that connection, with the notion of the *plērōma*, or fullness of man.

"The first creation" is of the whole of man, of humanity, i.e., of Adam. Adam is man, as species, not as individual. Gregory knows he is speculating and does not advance this as authoritative Christian teaching. He merely invites us to consider it, and begs leave "to place it in the form of a theoretical speculation before our kindly hearers."

In saying that God created man the text indicates, by the indefinite character of the term, all mankind. . . . The name given to the man created is not the particular [the proper], but the general name: thus we are led by the employment of the general name of our nature to some such view as this—that in the Divine foreknowledge and power all humanity is included in the first creation. . . . For the image is not

in part of our nature, nor is the grace in any one of the
things found in that nature, but this power extends
equally to all the race, and a sign of this is that mind
is implanted alike in all: for all have the power of
understanding and deliberating, and of all else
whereby the Divine nature finds its image in that
which was made according to it: the man that was
manifested at the first creation of the world, and he
that shall be after the consummation of all are alike,
they equally bear in themselves the Divine image.[68]

The corporate nature of mankind is what is in the image of
God. The separation into male and female and into individuals does not belong to the ultimate or original nature of man.
There is no marriage in heaven, the Scriptures teach us. There
is no individualism there either, let us hope.

One can easily dispose of this peculiar idea of Gregory by
ascribing it to Plato or Plotinus or Philo. But why does this
careful Christian thinker who rejects so much of Plato and
Plotinus stick to this one?

It seems to be closely linked with his notion of the Trinity.
In his essay On Not Three Gods, he says in effect: There is
one human nature, but many men. We say there is one *ousia*
in God but three *hupostaseis* ("hypostases"). But there are not
three Gods. The problem is that, according to Gregory, it is
also an abuse of language to say that there are many men.
Luke is a man, but not every man is Luke. Stephen is a man,
but not every man is Stephen. Yet the man in Luke and Stephen
is the same. They belong to the same nature. Man is the collective name for all. Plural in manifestation, yet the human
entity is one corpus. The parallel between the Trinity and
mankind may not be entirely appropriate. Yet primarily man
is one and only secondarily many individuals.

In our own time, the unity of humanity and the priority of
the corporate nature of man begin to become apparent. Gregory's statement of the issue may be inadequate. And yet in
developing an anthropology relevant to our time we cannot

ignore the notion of the primordial and ultimate unity of mankind. What God has foreseen and provided for mankind he has provided for the entire human race as it extends in time and space, "from Adam to parousia" as the liturgy phrases it. From the perspective of eternity where past, present, and future appear co-temporally or trans-temporally and where all space converges into a point, mankind is one and indivisible, even as God, whose image it is.[69]

Sexuality is the source of individuality. It was not in the original creation. It will disappear in the ultimate state of man. *Contra* Barth, Gregory insists that the image does not include sexuality.

MANKIND IN HISTORY

But sexuality, and consequently individuality, are not evil. They have their role to play in human historical development. Sexuality is the means that God provided in anticipation of human sin, and therefore of death, in order that mankind may multiply and attain to its *plērōma*, or fullness. Birth is thus the consequence of death, which in turn is the result of sin, and sexuality is necessary for birth and the full growth of mankind.

If death and birth are thus the consequence of sin, temporality may also be seen in the same light, for what is temporality except fixed duration between birth and death? The breakdown of the original unity of mankind thus appears as the current history of birth and death, of individual existence. Both are signs of the Fall, and the redemption of man has to lie beyond both. Yet that redemption comes only through temporal existence, through individual existence, through birth and death. The *plērōma*, or the fullness, of humanity is now to be achieved—quantitatively through birth and death, and qualitatively through individual achievements.

In the original creation there was no interval, no gap, no distance, between genesis and fulfillment, but in this historical existence, sin has introduced the interval (*diastēma*), the distance between what is and what ought to be. Man, both the individual and the race as a whole, has now to overcome temporality, gradually regaining the original unity and perfection.

Obviously, for modern theology, this is Gregory's weakest point, or so it would at first appear. What he has to say about history does not amount to very much. Modern man needs more place for history in his understanding of redemption. But let us understand Gregory further in his context before beginning to reconstruct our own "theology" for our time, out of the inspiration that he provides.

THE DESTINY OF MAN AND THE PENULTIMACY OF HELL

Time and sexuality are to pass away; the final destiny of man is to be one, eternal, immortal, in the resurrection. Then the *plērōma*, or fullness, of humanity will appear as Christ's own body, and that will be the completion of our deification. All evil is to be driven out. Eternal hell has no place in the final denouement, which is the total victory of good and the total banishment of evil. Evil had a beginning. It cannot be eternal. It must be banished in the end. The end of evil is the end of all that is to end, so that the good can endure.

Hell may have a penultimate function of purification of those who are still mixed with evil, but Gregory would have thought it rather Manichaean to regard evil, and therefore hell, as eternal and ultimate.

THE STRUCTURE OF FREEDOM AS "APATHEIA"

The freedom of man has certain functional aspects which it will be useful to clarify. We have already referred to two of these, namely, (a) absence of sexuality and (b) incorruptibility, or immortality, or freedom from birth and death.

The third functional element of human freedom, which Gregory calls *apatheia*, may best be translated "spiritual spontaneity," rather than passionlessness. Strictly speaking, in Gregorian vocabulary *pathos* stands for all that detracts man from the good. "The impulse which, with the participation of the will, goes from good to evil, is *pathos* properly so called." [70] But Gregory uses *pathos* also in another sense, namely, to denote our "tunics of skin," our mortal bodies, and *apatheia* thus stands for deliverance from evil as well as for deliverance from the "body of this death," as Paul calls it.

Apatheia has a positive sense as well. It is participation in the divine plenitude and spontaneity. It is to have equilibrium without losing dynamic force, to be able to move according to will and not be pushed from outside.

For the Stoic, *apatheia* meant the equilibrium of pure dispassionateness, the absence of all desire. For Gregory, on the other hand, since man has been made for the enjoyment of both the intelligible and the sensible worlds, the sheer absence of desire will not constitute freedom. The second chapter of On the Making of Man waxes poetically eloquent about all that God has made on earth for man's enjoyment.

> The rich and munificent Entertainer (the creator) of our nature, when he had decked the habitation (the earth) with beauties of every kind, and prepared this great and varied banquet, then introduced man, assigning to him as his task not the acquiring of what was not there, but the enjoyment of the things that were there, and for this reason he gives him as foundation the instincts of a two-fold organization, blending the divine with the earthy, that by means of both he may be naturally and properly disposed to each enjoyment, enjoying God by means of his more divine nature, and the good things of the earth by the sense that is akin to them. [71]

Apatheia for man is not dry asceticism, but the capacity to enjoy life in both its dimensions, the spiritual and the physical, but without losing one's equilibrium or becoming in bondage to the desire for sensual pleasures. Corporeal enjoyment is to be integrated into "spiritual" enjoyment, not replaced by it. *Eros* is to be integrated with *agapē*, not denied.

The three kinds of *apatheia* are all different. That of God comes from plenitude of power and good, from the infinity and indivisibility of a pure spirit. That of the angels is angelic, not related to the enjoyment of the things of this earth. That of man is a harmonious equilibrium of two opposing tendencies, one pulling up and one dragging down. It is a dynamic equilibrium, not a static passionlessness as in Stoicism. It is the continuous tension of the human spirit to find its true mode of being as the mediator between heaven and earth.

FREEDOM AS "PARRĒSIA"

Parrēsia as a Greek word has no English equivalent. In classical Greek it means frankness, forthrightness, courage, freedom of speech, fearless openness. In the New Testament the word plays a special role, as a consequence of the power of the Holy Spirit. In Mark 8:32, it was the Spirit that gave Jesus the boldness to say that the Son of Man must be killed. When Peter contradicted the bold words of the Spirit (for Jesus spoke the *logos* with *parrēsia,* says the text), he was sharply rebuked. In Acts 4:13, Peter and John speak with *parrēsia* as a result of Pentecost.

But *parrēsia* means also bold access into the presence of the Sovereign. According to Eph. 3:12, we have boldness (*parrēsia*) to enter into the presence of the sovereign God because of the Spirit. In Heb. 4:16 and 10:19 we are asked to draw near to the throne of grace with *parrēsia*. So also in I John 3:21 we learn that a clear conscience gives us *parrēsia* in relation to God.

This is also the meaning of the word for Gregory. A clear conscience and the presence of the Spirit make it possible for us to turn boldly and spontaneously toward God, and to enter his presence. This free access to God belongs to the original image, and the regaining of it is part of man's liberation.

To join the heavenly choir, to sing and to dance without worry and anxiety, to rejoice and again to rejoice—this is true liberty. The very nudity without shame of Adam and Eve belongs to this *parrēsia* and this freedom. Sin makes Adam and Eve hide when God comes to visit them. To be free means not to need to hide from God or from each other. Man's alienation from God and from his fellowmen, as well as from his own creations—this is sin. Freedom means the spontaneity with which we can deal with each other and with the creation, and the freedom with which we can rejoice in the presence of God.

Apatheia and *parrēsia* are not unrelated to each other. A clear conscience, a simple spontaneity, and a bubbling joy characterize both. This is the freedom of the image for which man longs.

FREEDOM AS "THEŌRIA"

If God is inaccessible and incomprehensible, how can we have freedom of access into his presence? Only because his presence extends into our world, not by *ousia* but by *energy*. It is in this energy that we are united with God and behold God. And again let us not forget that the cleansed and purified image is itself a mirror in which we can behold God in the interior of our very being.

Theōria is the capacity to behold God, not face to face, but as in a mirror. He who is the true image, Jesus Christ, himself became that mirror when he was transfigured on Mt. Tabor. To behold God and to rejoice in him is the very nature of the soul. *Apatheia* and *parrēsia* are correlate with *theōria*.

FURTHER ANALYSIS OF FREEDOM

The freedom of man, so central to Gregory's thought, has so far been analyzed in relation to God. Now it is time to see it in relation to the reality of the created order.

There are five characteristic words that Gregory uses to denote the freedom of man in this sense: *adoulotos, adespotos, autokratēs, autexousios,* and *eleutheros.* These words, often interchangeable, should be taken in their totality to understand the nature of man's freedom.

Adoulotos and *adespotos* are negative words, of political origin, denoting the free citizen in the Greek republics. Not the slave of another, not having a master—that is what they literally mean. Not someone who can be treated as a means to an end, as an instrument or a tool for someone else—that seems to be the meaning in context. If God is free and sovereign, then the image must also be treated as free and sovereign.

Autokratēs means the same thing as sovereign. Literally it means ruling and acting out of one's own power—a title reserved for the emperors. To be able to exercise power without external constraint, to be an uncaused cause, that would be the meaning in context. *Autexousios* means essentially the same thing—having authority in oneself, not acting on someone else's authority, not forced to act by necessity.

Eleutheria, the classical word for freedom, essentially means the absence of constraint, either external or internal, freedom from all enslavement and bondage to forces outside oneself, including the law, sin, death, etc., and also from the tyranny of the passions of the flesh. This freedom can only in part be realized on this earth, as long as we are in the flesh.

This unequivocal affirmation of the sovereignty and dignity of man is peculiar to the Eastern tradition, it seems. This freedom is what is distinctive of man and defines his nature—not original sin, or even being a creature, as it is often implied in the Western tradition. Man, despite his sin, is by nature in the image of God, and that is his destiny as well.

What happens to the doctrine of grace, if man is that independent? Gregory never seems to have raised the question. Was he then a Pelagian before Pelagius? Hardly—for the notion of grace as the goodwill of God acting within a lump of humanity which is totally evil, would have been abhorrent to Gregory. Augustine's doctrine of grace was the natural corol-

lary of his assumption that fallen man was totally evil and that
no movement toward the good could come from it.

Pelagius, as we have suggested, must have learned from
Nyssa, but was not deep enough to see where the real difference between Nyssa and Augustine lay.

SOME FURTHER ELEMENTS OF THE IMAGE RELEVANT TO OUR TIME

It is best simply to list these aspects of Gregory's thought in
summary fashion:

1. Man is made to rule, to be a king over creation. "Our
   nature was created to be royal from the first," says
   Nyssa. God is king. So is his image. It was made to rule
   the rest. It participates in God's kingship "in rank and
   in name."
2. Man is potentially capable of all good. In fact, "image
   of God" is shorthand for "capable of all good."
3. God is love. Man, as he conforms to God's image, manifests this love as the basic good. God is wisdom and
   power. So is man. Wisdom, power, and righteousness
   are aspects of the good.
4. Man is born destitute of natural weapons and protective
   covering, unlike the animals with brute strength. This
   is not a deficiency, for this means that man has both to
   develop his mind and to gain control over other animals
   and things by means of his mind. He can use his mind
   to control and use his environment, but also to make
   weapons and tools, clothes and shoes.
5. Man walks upright. This is part of the dignity of the
   image. It denotes his sovereignty. It also liberates his
   hands to become the instruments of his reason. The
   animals use their hands (forepaws) to support their
   bent head. Mans' use of his hands is part of his rational
   nature, along with speech and thought.
   Gregory is eloquent on this importance of man's up-

right posture and the use of the hands as essential elements in man's elevation from the rest of the animal world. This is a surprising insight in a fourth-century writer. The very intricate argument in Ch. VIII of On the Making of Man can only be summarized here. Because man stands upright, his posture becomes royal and dignified. His "forelegs" serve no longer to support the stooping body, but are liberated to be at the service of reason. We speak with our hands when we write. Nature makes advances through stages—inanimate nature, animate life, and then rational beings. And "hands are shown to be the property of the rational nature," for if the hands had not been released, man's head would have continued to stoop to the ground, "his lips would have projected from his mouth, lumpy, and stiff, and thick, fitted for taking up the grass, and his tongue would either have lain between his teeth, of a kind to match his lips, fleshy, and hard, and rough, assisting his teeth to deal with what came under his grinder" and thus the lips and the tongue would have been incapable of producing anything but bleatings or barkings. "But now, as the hand is made part of the body, the mouth is at leisure for the service of mind." [72]

6. Man has mind and reason. These are an aspect of the image, for God has mind and reason. So also is man's capacity for art and music. But the mind cannot be limited to just the brain or the heart, but extends over the whole human person. A healthy body and an active mind belong to the purity of the image.

7. The mind operates by the senses, and though it is something other than the senses, it is impossible to locate or to understand. The invisibility and incomprehensibility of the human mind is an aspect of the incomprehensibility and invisibility of its archetype—God. But in the case of man, soul and body have the same origin and are integral to each other in this life.

8. Man not only is made in the image of God, but he recapitulates in himself the cosmos—he is a microcosmos. He is also integrally related to the cosmos, not merely a prisoner of it. "It has been said by wise men that man is a little world in himself and contains all the elements which go to complete the universe." [73] Gregory further interprets this in his treatise On the Making of Man,[74] to draw an analogy between body, soul, and spirit in man and the vegetative, animal, and spiritual kingdoms in creation. Thus the redemption of man implies the redemption of the whole of creation.

Gregory of Nyssa thus provides us with an alternate structure within which to shape a Christian "ideology" adequate to our time. We need not fall into the dualism of the two cities, one of the earth and the other of God. Nor do we need to regard man as totally evil. Neither is it necessary to behold salvation by grace as something that happens primarily in and to the individual.

The adoption of such an alternate structure of Christian thought has many implications that are most significant for man's pursuit of his God-given destiny.

Take, for example, our understanding of the status of non-Christians in the presence of God (and also the related question—What difference does being a Christian make?). Within the Augustinian framework it is practically impossible to see how any non-Christian born after the time of Christ will have any choice but that of perishing eternally. When Augustine's contemporary, Nectarius of Calama, pointed out that some non-Christians seem to be more "virtuous" than many Christians, Augustine simply ignored the argument by calling the virtues of the pagans but "splendid vices." This was consistent with Augustine's frame of thought, which regards man as totally evil, and Christ and membership in his church as the only channel for grace.

In Gregory's way of thinking, creation itself is an act of

grace on the part of God. For what is grace after all? When God does something out of his free and abundant love, that is an act of grace. And creation is just as unmerited as redemption.

Seen in this perspective, even fallen man, insofar as he exists, exists by grace. If he were totally evil, he would not exist, but become pure nonbeing. Not merely man in his fallen state, but even the material and animal creations owe their origin to the grace of God, continue in existence by that grace and participate in the redemption in Christ by the same grace. All creation is to be redeemed and recapitulated in Christ. If even the nonhuman creation is to participate in the redemption achieved by Christ, what reason do we have to think that non-Christian humanity will perish totally and completely?

This line of argument which ensues from Gregory's thought is not to be confused with Origen's universalism. Origen's creation was composed of a fixed number of souls. Gregory's creation is a material-spiritual complex in which man, with his material body and corporate existence, is master. It is this whole universe with the whole of humanity that Christ came to redeem.

This again should not be assimilated into the old worn-out categories of thought and understood in the sense that "everybody will be saved, because God is good." Neither everybody nor everything will be saved. To be saved means to attain to deathless and evil-less being. But not every man, nor the whole of any man, nor the whole of everything will attain this. Only that which has become good can endure. That which is evil must experience dissolution and death. This means that the evil in Christians as well as in non-Christians is destined to be burned by fire. But that which is well pleasing to God—be it Christian or non-Christian, animal or material, art or music, act of kindness or thought of love—cannot perish. It will be gathered up into the kingdom. It is already there.

If this is the case, then being a Christian would make no difference at all, and the preaching of the gospel would be in vain, some may fear. Here again a proper solution of the problem is dependent on the categories we use. We may be used to thinking of people in terms of "saved" or "unsaved," though such categories are no longer used even by theologians these days. Our theological traditions, especially in that hideous era of Christian thought which was called the modern missionary era, often made that equation the basis of its thought: "Christian equals saved; non-Christian equals unsaved." So the Christian mission had as its objective to transform non-Christians into Christians.

There is, however, a more Christian way of thinking about what it means to be a Christian: A Christian is one who has been initiated into the community of the spirit, a community which exists on behalf of the whole of humanity, and which is being transfigured as it becomes an instrument of transfiguration for the whole of humanity, and in fact for all creation.

This understanding of Christianity does not say, "All religions are essentially the same—different roads leading to the same goal, namely, God." It does see the incarnate ministry of Jesus Christ as the centrally significant event for all of humanity and for all of history, but does not confine all the activity of Christ and the Holy Spirit to the church as separated from the rest of humanity.

It is possible to see the grace of God operating in the whole of creation. One must warn here against the tendency to assimilate these thoughts into the familiar Western categories of "natural law" or "natural revelation." Those categories have their roots in the basic dualism generated by Augustinian thought between nature and grace or between nature and supernature.

The frame of thought of the present writer is supplied by the conviction that the creation itself is a consequence and manifestation of the gracious will of God, and that therefore the grace of God is present and active in the whole of creation. Without grasping this, it will not be possible to come to terms with the ideas expressed here.

The acceptance of this axiom removes the barrier from the way to seeing the gracious activity of God in every aspect of creation—in other religions, in antireligious movements, in the life of animals and birds, even in the movement of "inanimate" matter which is aslo animated by the creative and gracious energy of God. This does not, however, mean that everything is all right, or that we do not have to make judgments between various religions or values. The life and teaching of Jesus Christ is still the norm and criterion for such evaluation. But this norm cannot be applied in some impersonal, objective, scientific, way. It can be applied only by communities and individuals who are being transfigured into the image of God. The criterion is therefore twofold: (1) a subjective transformation of the person making the judgment, and (2) the objective teachings and example of our Lord.

The liberation of man spiritually from his anxieties and insecurities is a primary precondition to gaining perspective on other religions and so-called secular phenomena. A theological framework that aids in this liberation, without forcing us to sacrifice the fundamental Christian affirmations, as the secular gospel of yesterday asked us to do, needs to be examined in all seriousness by all intelligent Christians, even if theologians may take a couple of decades to catch on to it. Theological liberation, in a truly transcendent sense, not in the false secular sense, is an integral part of the liberation of man, especially Christian man.

CHAPTER V
The Liberation of Man

Where is man going?

Wherever he goes, he had better start where he is.

The last third of the twentieth century is where he seems to be. The second half of this century has certainly, so far at least, been the half-century of the liberation of man. Will it also be the half-century of man's attainment of freedom? For freedom is surely more than liberation. It includes man's becoming man. Liberation only places us on the threshold of freedom.

Six Movements Toward Liberation

Since mid-century, liberation has taken six forward steps, and thus brought mankind closer to the threshold of freedom.

The first forward step of liberation came as our half-century began, with political decolonialization. The Philippines, India, Burma, Pakistan, Ceylon, and Indonesia were among the first to break loose. Gandhi, Nehru, Jinnah, Sukarno, and others became the symbols of a new hope of human dignity for all. A decade or so later, Africa followed suit. Emancipation brought a wild excitement and a new vitality to the repressed people of the dark continents. One billion five hundred mil-

lion people broke their political chains, and marched with a
new confidence into the wide arena of world reality.

In the light of continuing economic enslavement, political
emancipation proved a heady wine that brought on the head-
aches that often go with the sobriety of the morning after.

The second step of emancipation soon followed, however—
the awakening of Negro self-consciousness in the Afro-Ameri-
can peoples. The sit-ins and the bus boycotts snowballed to
become Black Power and the defiance of white superiority. It
was again the Son of Man waking up to snap the shackles that
bound him.

The third movement begins to break another bond—that of
socialist dictatorship. Yugoslavia pioneered. Hungary tried to
break her fetters, but was mercilessly rebound. So did Czechoslovakia in more recent times. But the real liberation is going
on in another quarter—in the realm of ideas.

It began perhaps in 1956 with the revolt of the Polish and
the Hungarian Marxist writers. Gomulka's apparently effective
repression of the revolt in Poland was, however, not by any
means the end of the story. Polish writers continued to insist
even on March 14, 1964, on the point made by the young Marx
in 1842: "The free press is the manifestation of the vigilance
of spirit of a people, the expression of their self-confidence,
the link that relates the person to the State and to the world." [75]
The letter of the thirty-four Polish writers against censure led
only to further intimidation and repression.

Those writers have refused to give up. In other socialist
countries, including Russia, open letters from writers began to
appear. The new martyrs of literature became the heroes of
the socialist underground. In February, 1968, the Polish writers
again spoke up when the government forbade the continuing
performance of the play *Dziady*. The extraordinary session of
the Writers Association Conference on February 29 saw a bold
resolution against government censure received with furtive
but widespread applause. Many senior writers spoke out with
unprecedented audacity against the "creatures in dotage" who

suppressed the dignity of Polish literature. Mr. Gomulka, whose formal education did not go far beyond the primary level, soon took repressive measures against the intellectual rebels, charging them with anti-Soviet and anti-Party activities.

In the Soviet Union itself a whole new mode of communication has sprung up. On its face it does not appear subversive or revolutionary. The Russian who comes across this underground literature can, however, read between the lines a critique of contemporary Soviet society that is both trenchant and perceptive. This typed literature copied and distributed from hand to hand establishes links between human beings that confirms each in his or her own opposition to the communist establishment. Some of it is obviously the airing of private gripes. Much of it, however, has a cumulative effect in reinforcing a widespread network of opposition to the current regime. Leonid Brezhnev, in his address to the 24th Congress of the Communist Party in the Soviet Union (April, 1971), made it clear that he was aware of this resistance and was going to deal with it firmly but without fanfare. No doubt we are going to see a time of even greater restriction on personal liberties in the Soviet Union, which would go hand in hand with a more abundant supply of consumer goods. On the other hand, there can be little doubt that the thaw has to come sooner or later, when Communism itself will enter a new phase in seeking and achieving the liberation of man.

There is a new vitality in the literature of the communist societies, which, because it is an upsurge of human freedom, cannot be ultimately repressed.

One is not naïve enough to think that all who revolt against communist dictatorship do so in the cause of authentic freedom. Many may be already too much attracted by the successes of the bourgeois West which they would like to emulate. But there is no doubt that the two great historic structures denying human freedom—the Roman Catholic Church and the Communist Party—are both experiencing earth tremors which forebode at least an eruption, if not a major quake.

A fourth and perhaps most significant chain that is being broken is that of the authority of the older generation. Youth in revolt has never been so radical and so powerful. Student rebellions were first introduced into politics in the present writer's memory, by the "Quit India" resolution in 1942. Students were encouraged by political leaders to protest against colonial oppression. Now that same protest has grown in a quarter century to proportions that alarm political leaders as much as university administrators. The year 1967–1968 saw student protests in Argentina, Belgium, Berlin, Brazil, Britain, Colombia, Congo Kinshasa, Czechoslovakia, France, West Germany, East Germany, Ethiopia, India, Indonesia, Ireland, Japan, Korea, Lebanon, Malaysia, Mexico, the Netherlands, Nigeria, Pakistan, Poland, South Africa, Spain, Tunisia, Turkey, and the United States.

The most significant of these may be the American, the French, and the Polish-Czechoslovakian protests. The events in France that began with the student revolt at the University of Nanterre on March 22, 1968, are regarded by the French as the most important political development since 1871, if not since 1848. Students took to the barricades again in their fight against an oppressive establishment. May 11, 1968, saw Paris rocked to its bottom by student revolt. It is a revolt against the magisterial authority of the professor and the administrator, a demand for freedom for the student to choose what he should learn and how he should live while at the university.

The student revolt has already begun to fulfill the predictions of some of its adverse critics. It was essentially or at least in large part a bourgeois revolt, and two of the characteristics common among members of the bourgeoisie, or middle class, are their love of comfort and their lack of staying power in the face of adverse circumstances. In the United States, for example, there was a new upsurge of revolt following the speech and action of President Nixon extending the Vietnam War to Cambodia and Laos. American students expressed considerable naïveté in fondly hoping that a few demonstrations, a few letters and telegrams to congressmen, and a few more liberal Democrats in Congress would end the war in Indochina.

The student protest as a whole has lacked any adequate structure or clearly defined goals which could inspire and harness the energies of the majority of the student population. Few students are prepared to risk their careers or to jeopardize their own stake in the establishment. Since the students involved have generally been unwilling to pay the price of sacrifice and suffering, unable to create structures for the changing of society, unprepared to discipline themselves in and for a tough struggle with the powers of injustice and dehumanization, their protest in its present form shows little promise for the future. But there are new forms emerging.

Youth have begun to pioneer in certain significant directions. Especially notable are the communes and the counter culture syndrome. The communes are experimental communities of young and older couples. They are mostly people from the city who seek to break out of the frontiers of the nuclear family by joining a voluntary community that includes males and females of all ages, old people as well as children. Their hope is to provide some more intimate community support for the individual, and greater capacity to contain and overcome tensions between individuals through the ability of the small community to provide alternate relationships. Such relationships can ease tensions and also furnish a third-party presence that can prevent the tensions from breaking out into aggression. There is also an element of romanticism in the communes, a sort of "back to nature" movement reminiscent of Rousseau. The viciously polluted spiritual and physical atmosphere of the city today makes the desire to escape from it more understandable than in Rousseau's time. But it is difficult to see these communes as the essential elements of the way forward when (a) not all people can afford the luxury of leaving the city, and (b) the communes often attract people who are seeking to escape not only from the city but also from their own distorted selves. They are significant, however, as a protest against the urban-technological civilization and as a search for more spontaneous community.

Fifth, the Roman Catholic Church has been the last bastion of authority. The authority of the pope as Pastor Universal was considered beyond question by intelligent Roman Catholic theologians until a few years ago. Even after the Vatican Council, Pope Paul VI managed to assume an authoritarian role that seemed to go against the spirit of the Council. However, when he boldly and with incredible audacity spoke in his *Humanae Vitae* against the practice of artificial birth control, the worldwide reaction to it seemed to promise a new upsurge of intellectual and moral freedom within the bosom of the Catholic Church. Catholic bishops and theologians are now openly encouraging disobedience to papal authority.

The revolt against authority in the Roman Catholic Church also may take unexpected directions. The debate between Karl Rahner and Hans Küng, two prominent European Catholic theologians, bids fair to mark the most crucial stage in the post-Vatican II struggle against concentration of authority in the Roman Church. When Rahner wrote in the *Stimmen der Zeit* a scathing review of Küng's massive attack on papal infallibility,[76] the whole theological world took note. For to put the book and the review together is to come up against an interesting paradox that reveals the deepest issues in the problem of authority.

The gist of Küng's book is that the infallibility of the church, a late arrival in Catholic dogma, has no theological justification. What could be defended, according to him, is the *indefectibility* of the church as a whole and in the long term. Küng argues, as I have done for decades, that only God is infallible. But God has promised the church that the Spirit would guide it into all truth. So even if the church as a whole or a particular teaching authority in it may go wrong at a particular point in history on a particular matter, the Spirit will lead the church back to the truth.

Küng's thesis is indeed a far cry from the assertion that when the bishop of Rome has pronounced formally on matters relating to faith and ethics, he cannot go wrong. It is quite different from the view that no one has the authority to question the formal ethical dicta and dogmatic teaching proclaimed by the pope on his own authority (and not from the consensus of the church).

The paradox arises from the question which Rahner has raised in his review: "It becomes hard to treat him [i.e., Küng] any longer as a Catholic. . . . One can only carry on a discussion with Küng as one would with a liberal Protestant." The Roman Catholic Church officially requires that a person accept the dogma of papal infallibility in order to be a Catholic. Has not Küng ceased to be a Catholic by denying that doctrine?

The further question is, On what authority does Küng attack the doctrine of authority taught in the Roman Catholic Church? It would appear that it is the authority of Scripture that Küng accepts as *norma normans*, and here Rahner is right in calling Küng a Protestant, for the doctrine of Scripture as the finally normative authority belongs mainly to the Protestant tradition and is characteristic of it. But I suspect that there will be Roman Catholic theologians who could question the doctrine of papal infallibility without necessarily accepting Scripture as the final norm. When that happens, we shall have entered a new phase in Western religious thought.

What is certain is that the structure of authority patiently built up by the Roman Catholic Church ever since the time of Leo the Great in the fifth century, and strongly reinforced in the period after the Council of Trent in the sixteenth, seems today to be crumbling. This should be regarded as a step forward in the march of freedom. For while it is true that during this very period between the fifth and twentieth centuries, the period of development of Western Christianity, the church has produced some of the greatest thinkers and spiritual leaders of the West, by and large the authority structure in the church has stood in the way of freedom's advance. That obstacle is now being removed.

Sixth, the women's liberation movement—or "women's lib," as it has come to be called, sometimes affectionately, at other times glibly with a superior smile from uncomprehending males—is potentially one of the most liberating movements of our time. Women are more than half of mankind, and there can be little doubt that in social, political, and economic organizations the males have generally been at the helm. Exceptions could be pointed out in the form of matriarchal societies in certain tribes or the "market mammies" of West Africa who play a dominant economic role, but the fact remains that these are exceptions. The rule is still male domination in public decision-making and in the use of economic and political power. Neither do women prime ministers in India, Ceylon, and Israel disprove the general rule.

But it is not without significance that it is in Asian and African societies that women are able to come to the top more easily than in Western countries. In some Western countries, such as Switzerland and Belgium, women until recently still lagged behind their non-Western sisters in achieving the right to vote.

The women's liberation movement often claims that the oppression of women is as old as human history. This is true only in the sense that most forms of oppression and exploitation of one class of human beings by another are as old as humanity. It is the social conditions peculiar to an individualistic, urban-technological civilization and that strange phenomenon, the nuclear family, which goes with that civilization, that have thrown into relief the oppression of women as a class. Small wonder, then, that in the West the movement for women's liberation dates from the earlier half of the nineteenth century, when the urban-technological civilization begins to blossom and in the nuclear family one man and one woman are forced to work out their relationships without the checks and balances provided by the larger family unit composed of at least three generations and several cousins and in-laws.

The 1840's were also the period of revolt against the exploitation of women and children as cheap labor in the appalling conditions provided by the factories of that time. Women's liberation then was part of the revolt against the new middle-class, male establishment that was coming into a dominant role in the West during this period. Male intellectuals were ready at hand to provide men with the ideological structure necessary to justify their continued domination and exploitation of women. Everything the domineering male middle class wanted for itself could be *reified* ("made into things"), and even woman began to become "property."

The revolt of Western women in the mid-nineteenth century failed to enlist support from even a significant minority of women, and male chauvinism as expressed in the writings of Nietzsche and Schopenhauer triumphed for the moment. These two, along with less well known writers like Otto Weininger, were among the most blunt and blatant in their antifeminism, but subtler forms of the denigration of woman appeared in much of the literature of the time. Today the mass media have become the most effective instruments for blotting out the voice of the women's liberation movement, or else of caricaturing and lampooning it and seeking to render it innocuous. Of course any passionate movement of revolt is certain to provide plenty of material for funny cartoons or uncomprehending satire.

The tendency to glorify masculine manhood continues to be prevalent in our time in the writings of Hemingway, D. H. Lawrence, and even Kazantzakis, the apostle of freedom. The great attraction that the idea of violence and aggressive action holds for many minds in our time could also be related to this exaltation of virility and adventurousness.

Perhaps the fact that women's liberation as a movement originated in America has its own significance. Though the fascist regimes of Hitler and Mussolini were even more violently aggressive, these dictators had taken care to see that no movement of any kind of liberation would raise its head within their domain. America combines large-scale, violent aggression with a great measure of personal freedom that was totally absent in the fascist regimes. Some such effect is conceivable, therefore, as that in Aristophanes' *Lysistrata*, where it was the women who finally forced the dominant male Athenians and Spartans to agree to lay down their arms.

The women's liberation movement holds within it the germs of perhaps the most significant psychic revolution in the history of mankind. The human psyche is mainly a creation of history. In the case of man and woman, there has been a division, not merely of labor, but also of virtues. But the labor and the virtues were not unrelated to each other. Biology and society worked together to assign certain tasks to women like child-rearing and housekeeping, while men were to be gatherers of goods and fighters for defense or aggression. The so-called "female" virtues of passivity, compassion, tenderness, and even imagination came to be regarded as nonmasculine, while aggression, domination, acquisition by force, adventurousness, and ruthlessness became exalted as "male" virtues.

We thus live in a world made by men who regard these latter as the high values. Who else but women can teach men again that compassion and tenderness, poetry and imagination, are human virtues and not merely feminine? The effect of the women's liberation movement may eventually be that as more and more women begin to assume their legitimate share of the responsibility for making public decisions, the value system of both female and male humanity will undergo some drastic changes hard to predict at this time. It may aslo entail a radical change in human consciousness in general, paving the way for building a genuinely human society with justice and peace for all.

These six revolts against authority—against political colonialism, white supremacy, and socialist dictatorship, against the intellectual establishment, ecclesiastical authority, and male domination, are all far from consummated. Only when these movements of our half-century attain full force and courage can we say that we are reaching the threshold of freedom. We are still in the negative phase of freedom—that of liberation from bondage.

Four Errors to Be Protested

Even at this point there are issues still to be clarified. There is an intellectual task to be accomplished before mankind can march forward to the attainment of freedom. As the French say, in 1789 the people took the Bastille. On May 13, 1968, they "took the word" (*la prise de parole*) in the "capture" of the Sorbonne by student radicals. The days of detached academic neutrality are over, they claim. Mankind, through a limited number of pioneering youth, has swung into an upsurge of the poetic consciousness. Words now come from the heart, charged with feeling, not numbed with cerebration.

For the moment this poesy, this creative use of the word, remains a cry of protest more than a picture of the future. But in that seed of protest are the genes and chromosomes that shall in large part determine the future. Four aspects of this protest are well worth heeding.

1. *Law and Order.* First there is the protest against the absolutization of law and order. At its more superficial level, the three candidates in the American presidential election of 1968 all had to use this guarantee of law and order as their central platform in appealing for the votes of the American public. And it is not merely in economically well established societies that we see this inordinate regard for law and order, even at the expense of the claims of justice and dignity. In less-developed countries such as India, where the forces of linguistic and communal parochialism threaten to rend the hard-won unity of the nation, the cry for a strong police seems to sway the public.

At a more sophisticated level, people such as Prof. André Philip of France have been arguing that revolutions belong only to the past, and if in the underdeveloped countries some people are still dreaming and talking of revolution, they will soon be cured of it when they become more advanced, as European societies are.

He seems to argue that the technological era does not permit wholesale revolution, but can only promote piecemeal change. First there is the element of cost. The machinery of production has been put up at such great cost, and to ask for it to be overthrown by revolution is foolish, according to Professor Philip.[77] Second, technology in itself implies a built-in machinery for change. Our technological society will therefore need no revolutions.

How utopianly bourgeois a dream that is! The way in which bourgeois love of comfort, and therefore of law and order, distorts human reasoning seems simply incredible. Whatever be the cost, when men are being destroyed in their freedom and dignity by a system, that system has to be overthrown, for no system is as valuable as man. To bring in the issue of cost is perhaps symptomatic of what is happening to human values in Western society. However much built-in machinery for change a technological society may have, the use of such machinery is in the hands of those in power. The oppressed cannot simply wait until those in power feel well disposed enough to do some research into their problems, and propose some remedies at minimum cost to the holders of power.

This absolutization of a particular system of law and order is one of the great idolatries of Western liberal and conservative alike.

Planned change within the given structure of law and order, sometimes romantically termed "change by constitutional means," does take place in all societies whether in Russia or America, Cuba or Korea. To cease to change would be to ossify and die.

But constitutional change cannot always unseat a class from the throne of power. In many Latin American countries, for example, it is becoming increasingly clear that the political machinery is completely controlled by the economically dominant class, often allied to North American investors. North American exploitation of the economy of Latin America favors this ruling class while it progressively impoverishes the masses. Those who control economic and political power cannot be expected to introduce the necessary changes by constitutional means, for this would in effect deprive them of their power. To justify such a political and economic structure in the name of law and order is to reveal a bestial insensitivity to the sufferings of the oppressed and exploited.

The Christian faith affirms that the present structure of law and order is a human creation, and is not to be absolutized. It should be questioned, examined, and if found to be an oppressive idol, should be overthrown, even if that brings the roof of the temple over our heads. This is the spirit of the student protest. Law and order as a structured pattern of living indeed seems to be God-given; but no particular system is. Even the revolutionary and the guerrilla have their own law and order. No society can long survive without some form of law and order.

The particular system of law and order in which we live, if found inadequate to the needs of fostering human freedom and dignity, will have to be overhauled. An alienated system of law and order, over which man is powerless, and which continues to dicate to him against his own better judgment, certainly has become demonic.

2. *Violence.* A second intellectual error persists in our societies in relation to the issue of violence and nonviolence.

By violence we mean the use of excessive strength against the will of another to produce injury or damage to person or property.

The word "revolution" creates many negative reactions in peoples' minds, mostly because of its association with violence. But revolution need not imply broken skulls, machine guns, and bloodbaths. We speak of the industrial revolution, the technological revolution, and the cybernetic revolution, when all we mean is a radical change in the means of production and distribution. These revolutions entail a chain reaction of sweeping change in human social relations and living conditions.

What most men fear seems to be political revolution. Here we mean the application of force to change the seat of power against the will of those in power. Not all political revolutions are violent in character. The Greek military junta took over power in 1967 with a minimum of skull-breaking and bloodbaths. It was a revolution, even if the junta in power remains a reactionary force in most respects.

But the application of excessive strength to cause injury or damage to persons and property need not always be clearly visible. Damage can be done to human persons by a system which on the surface appears nonviolent. Such damage is more subtle because we can more clearly see and more readily react against physical damage to human bodies and property than we can against damage to the dignity, freedom, and humanity of people. The excessive power used is not physical but economic and technological.

Most of our present systems of political and economic organization are oppressive and destructive of human dignity. Violence is endemic, built into the system, wherever big business or the landed aristocracy concentrates power in its own hands and uses that power to control the government of the people. Wherever justice is denied to the weak, wherever the dignity of man is violated, wherever people are forced into the slums or reduced to subhuman standards of living, in such societies violence is entrenched in the system itself. Constitutional change may be inadequate in such cases to deal with the problem in its fundamentals. Violent revolution or the forcible overthrow of those in power against their will may be the only means available for redressing the violence endemic in the system.

To refuse to support such revolution on the ground that violence is not Christian involves us in the dilemma that by our very refusal we are supporting the violence inherent in the system. We are in such a case confronted with a choice between two evils. Here a man's sensitive Christian conscience finds it difficult to make an easy decision that would keep his hands clean.

The Christian, however, cannot be so naïve as to think that simply by choosing to apply violence against the violent system, one has found the solution to the problem. Violence has its own nemesis, as we so well know these days. It is not possible to use hatred and violence as tools of regaining self-esteem and dignity, without having a price to pay. It is much cleaner to die as a martyr in the course of a revolutionary struggle than to win that struggle and ascend to the seat of power. For in the very application of violence to others, one becomes changed within oneself. Violence and the refusal to forgive destroy the humanity of man.

The Christian revolutionary has to exercise severe self-discipline in order to be fit to enter the revolutionary struggle. Certain elementary principles have to be observed. He should be pure in his motivation. He does not enter the struggle either to escape from the complications of his own personal life, or to wreak a personal vendetta on individuals or the class in power that has done him wrong. His motivation has to be participation in God's compassion for the oppressed and the downtrodden, and a genuine desire to see a just society in which even the erstwhile oppressor, properly chastened, can play his part in dignity.

He cannot seek power for the sake of power or for lording it over others. He has to share the poverty and suffering of the oppressed, and to sacrifice his own property and comfort for the sake of the revolutionary struggle. This is where the Christian liberal often becomes a hypocrite—in the inconsistency between his profession of solidarity with the poor and his practice of a level of living not within the means of the poor.

Even after coming to power in a victorious struggle, the Christian has to continue to be unsparing of himself, and to remain disciplined, willing to undergo hardship for the sake

of building up a society of justice. He refuses to accept
privilege and comfort as the prize for his unselfish efforts. He
continues to be a cross-bearer to the very end, always willing
to forgo his own interests in the interest of the people whom
he serves. The decision to enter a revolutionary struggle thus
involves for the Christian a momentous decision to walk the
way of the cross to the very end, expecting neither comfort
nor applause in return for his sacrifice.

One thing seems clear. We are essentially wrong if we
assume that we can walk into the heaven of freedom without
a struggle. The smooth, comfortable passage to a utopia
through technology and constitutional government is a bourgeois liberal dream which has no Christian content. The whole
gospel is the message of a continuing battle with the forces
of evil. The principalities and powers ranged against the
Prince of Peace will not be conjured away by parliamentary
speech-making, democratic electioneering, and technological
jugglery. They are determined to stay entrenched and give
battle till the end, when the day of the Lord shall dawn.

3. *The Urban Paradise.* A third mistaken assumption underlying much of our thinking as Christians is that the kingdom
of God is some form of urban-technological civilization, a
"secular city" spread worldwide.

Our age is already being called, among other things, the
"post-city age." The traditional city is fast disappearing. Our
pragmatic approach to life had once thought that a worldwide network of interconnected cities would be the cure for
most of our social ills. "The City Is Dead—Long Live the
City" is the title of a publication in 1966 of the Center for
Planning and Development Research at the University of
California, Berkeley. The city is a spatial entity, spatially
organized. But communications have been developing so fast,
that geography is almost being overcome. The urban-rural
distinction is becoming increasingly difficult to maintain. A
kind of national urban society seems to be emerging in most

Western countries as well as in Japan. We may be on the way to building a planet-wide cosmopolis. Some form of international community has already begun to take shape. Many regard themselves not as permanently belonging to any particular city or nation, but as citizens of the world, sharing in a cosmopolitan culture. The planet is their city and nation. These men are already the ordinary men of tomorrow, when the world will be just one great city.

Rarely does one hear a questioning of this line of optimistic thinking. The society of the girded loin, a nation of universal conquistadores, we are out to build a brave new world, where we shall all live happily ever after. In this urban-technological paradise we shall all be "free"—i.e., able to say, "I am my own man," and, "I can do my own thing." This unusual blend of universal urban-technological collectivism and a stupendously romantic individualism often form the substance of our notion of salvation.

> What we have perfected is technology, and it is technology on which most men, most places, most times, rest such vague hopes as still stir. It is now in or almost in our hand to feed lavishly, clothe, and render "literate" the world, to live in virtually instantaneous, ubiquitous, "communication," to annihilate nearly all physical distance, to command more energy than we can use, to engineer mood and perhaps perception at will, to write such genetic prescriptions as we wish, to make such men as whim may dictate. The universe capitulates. We are everywhere triumphant. But a premonitory smell of cosmic Neroism is in the air, and the cry of "stop the world; I want to get off" has become, whether absurd or not, pervasive and insistent.[78]

Not as pervasive and insistent as one wishes, you might like to say to the dean of the Center for the Study of Democratic Institutions in Santa Barbara, California. Most intellectuals, especially theologians, continue to be naïve and utopian in their hopes of the secular city and the technological paradise. Mastering facts by research, planning, program- ming, engineering, executing, evaluating, feedbacking, reno- vating, we merrily march our way to progress, only to find that we have lost ourselves along the way.

And that is what the hippie is protesting against. Freedom does not come by the mere external control of reality. The hippie knows it almost as well as did Gregory of Nyssa in the fourth century. One has to "find one's head," to *be*, to make sure that one *is*, even when one has stopped doing and started resting.

Man cannot *be*, just by doing, and by doing it for one's own advantage, and by doing what others expect of us or force us into doing. In our search for freedom, we have to seek more than the control of external reality. We cannot afford to lose ourselves in the process of gaining mastery of the universe.

> For what benefit is it to man, if he gains the whole
> cosmos while losing his own soul? Or what can he
> provide as substitute for his own soul? (Matt. 16:26.)

"Being one's own man" calls for more than "doing one's own thing." Gregory of Nyssa had already made clear that any mastery of the universe unaccompanied by a mastery of one's own self, cannot lead to true *eleutheria*, or freedom. Only when the *hēgemonikon*, or the ruling element within ourselves, is in full control of our minds and bodies, do we genuinely taste freedom. It is this aspect of freedom which is now in danger of being neglected even by theologians. The subconscious, unconscious, and conscious elements of fear and anxiety, guilt and aggression, boredom and purposelessness, need to be overcome in order to regain authentic humanity. The kingdom of God is much more complex than the secular city and the urban-technological paradise.

4. *A "Necessary" God.* A fourth prevailing misconception in much of our theological reflection relates to our attempts to find a relevant doctrine of God. The God of the gaps, of

the "necessary hypothesis," is of course dead or dying. There is a new tendency to affirm that God is nothing more than simply the destiny of man. Hegel had suggested that God is becoming, that he is in process of evolution, within the time-process. This is now translated into more secular terms to suggest that it is man who ultimately becomes God. A Marxist atheist such as Roger Garaudy would say that what Christians call their God is nothing but the exigency in man to become born as truly man.

In theology itself man-language and God-language are becoming quite interchangeable, the former tending to replace the latter. The difference between many so-called "atheists" and some so-called "believers" is, in Garaudy's happy phrasing, simply that for atheists there is no externally guaranteed promise of human fulfillment, while for believers there is such a promise. If the freedom of man requires that he be liberated from subservience to an external God, there are two possibilities. For secular man it is man's accepting full responsibility for his own existence and for the shape of the world. For many Christians, it is to have God as the depth or ground of our own being, so that it is God in us, operating through our thought, will, and action, who finally shapes the destiny of man.

It is in this attempt to capture God within human immanence that there lurks a great danger for human destiny. Here we are in a sense pushed back to Schleiermacher's immanent God and the resultant superficial liberalism. We need to maintain the otherness of God and divine immanence in some form of dialectical tension, not conceptually resolved, but maintained in a cultic milieu. Without that cultic acknowledgment of God's divine otherness as well as his union with us in the Eucharist, we become reductionists and at that point become sub-Christian, which means also subhuman.

We cannot achieve any adequate conceptual formulation of this dialectic between the otherness and the "in-us-ness" of God. The only adequate vehicle for maintaining it is in the

Eucharistic act, which itself should not be reduced to some facile notion of a Lord's supper where the "Lord" gives a banquet to all comers. It remains a mystery, and its character as a mystery, which brings the otherness of the trans-temporal and the trans-logical to the historical and the conceptual, needs to be maintained through proper discrimination. Else it is reduced to the level of the banal, as the Bible has already been so reduced through its indiscriminate use by all according to the whim and fancy of each.

To maintain the dignity and majesty of God against his despisers and would-be tramplers of his glory is a precondition for maintaining the dignity and majesty of man. When God becomes reduced to the level of empirical or even transcendent man, then empirical man's dignity and freedom can be too easily trampled upon by other men.

The mystery of the cosmos and man—realities subsisting within the trans-spatio-temporal world of intratrinitarian reality, maintained trans-conceptually in the Eucharistic rhythm of the church—this may appear utter nonsense to many minds; but to those who have experienced this world, such derision only convokes compassion. "Father, forgive them, for they know not what they do [or say]."

These four protests—(1) against absolutization of any given system of law and order, (2) against the condoning of violence in the system by the condemnation of revolutionary violence, (3) against the reduction of the kingdom of God to an urban-technological paradise, and (4) against the reduction of God to a radical immanentism—have within them indications of the way forward. And these we have to see further. None of these are automatic processes, like the six movements toward liberation that we discussed earlier in this chapter. To protest against these four errors calls for the utmost human vigilance. The protesting of these errors is much too feeble today to be heard widely. In fact, the four errors being protested are too widely proclaimed and too facilely accepted by many who have clear minds. Most modern theology makes at least two and sometimes all four of these errors. The theologians absolutize law and order or at least make it a higher priority than justice; they condemn or condone violence without qualification and without grasping its complexities; they are overoptimistic about the possibilities of our urban-technological civilization; and they do not see the relevance of the transcendence of God and the transcendence of man which is dependent upon it.

THE LIBERATION OF MAN AND THE BREAKTHROUGH IN GENETICS AND SPACE EXPLORATION

The liberation of man was confronted with new possibilities when the earth and its atmosphere as confining boundaries for human existence were broken through in the space-research achievements of the last third of our century. The earth with its field of gravity was no longer to be the sole domain of man's existence. Man's most common dream—to float in space without being held down by gravity—was no longer a mere dream. Of course we have not yet got very far beyond the earth and its satellite, but it is conceivable that within a short time after these pages go to press man will have set foot on other planets in the solar system. Once that is achieved, man cannot be expected to stop with the solar system. Theoretically there is no reason why he should not wander around to interstellar space and to other planetary systems belonging to other stars.

This breakthrough has consequences for the human consciousness which go far beyond the idea of geographical conquest. Our children are growing up with a world view quite different from the one with which our own generation did. It will be easier for the man of tomorrow to be liberated in his consciousness from a confining geocentrism and to conceive of man's vocation as extending far beyond the confines of this earth. His consciousness will soon have also to grapple with some of the problems connected with the nature of space itself.

What is space? Is it really uniform and bounded as we once thought? Is it in a constant or inconstant state of expansion? Does it have a center and a periphery? Where are we ourselves and our little solar system located in terms of these center–periphery axes? Is there some way of man transcending space itself, so that all space appears to him as "here" rather than divided into "here," "there," and "elsewhere"? The same or similar questions are sure to be put by the consciousness of man in relation to the nature of time. Space and time, the two great mysteries (i.e., logically inexplicable entities that cannot be conceptually grasped through our normal categories), form the warp and woof, the background of our existence. Space and time will themselves soon be seen by man in a fresh way, thus marking another stage in the liberation of man.

For man is, in the Christian vision, a visitor in time-space. The earth is not his natural or ultimate habitat. His home is heaven, the presence of his father and maker, God. And it is essential for the true liberation of man that he develop a state of consciousness in which time-space is seen also as a laboratory given to man in which to experiment with reality, or as a training ground for developing certain skills necessary for life in a totally different milieu. This is not to say that historical existence is meaningless. I do, however, mean that historical existence is meaningless by itself. History, like man, has to derive its significance from a realm outside of itself. Time-space does not belong to the ultimate nature of reality, but only to its phase in relation to the mind of man at a somewhat primitive stage of its development.

Perhaps it is quite stupid of me to find the significance of our contemporary achievements in space exploration, in these misty realms of the consciousness of man. Why not see these more concretely as the conquest of larger tracts of real estate to be dominated and used by man as he feels restless on this

overcrowded planet? Yes, of course, why not? But then I am
not a real-estate dealer, nor am I obsessed by ideas of geographical expansionism. The breakthroughs in science and
technology could be viewed either from the perspective of
their commercial value or, more wisely, in terms of how they
are used to transmute the environment of man and thereby
man himself.

Technology has now made that astounding breakthrough of
the elements of the genetic code, which opens the way to
shape the mind of man by direct action on the tissues that
bear and generate the mental processes. DNA (deoxyri-
bonucleic acid), the magic substance of the genes which contains the coded instructions for the growth and development
of each organism, has now been isolated and its structure
analyzed. The most spectacular aspect of that genetic breakthrough is the prospect of genetic surgery which not only can
remove inherited imperfections at the level of the genes
but claims the ability even to "create" superman to order by
doctoring up the genes—bigger and better brains, eyes, ears,
hands, or whatever else you choose.

This is all neither fable nor science fiction. A real possibility is opening up to man, the full brunt of which man has
still not faced. *Future Shock,* as a much-discussed book is
titled, will be painful for humanity, for the future is full of
shocking possibilities. Among these are the possibilities of
feeding information or language skills directly into the brain,
of simulating unheard-of pleasures by electronic stimulation
of certain parts fo the brain, the possibility of aggression control by electronic impulses, even the possibility of creating
life by chemical synthesis. These possibilities stagger the
mind and, when realized, will confront man with choices
so momentous and yet so far beyond the present level of the
maturation of human wisdom to undertake that they may very
well paralyze man into a state of cynical irresponsibility.

The Christian faith, especially as it conceives of man as
man in the image of God inheriting all the power, love, and

wisdom at the disposal of the Creator, does not allow man to be staggered or shocked by these possibilities, nor does it advise him to run away from them. Every new possibility that opens up before man confirms his basic faith that God wants to hold back nothing at all from his children. Everything that God can do, man can do also, except to be his own creator. The only problem is that there has to be some co-ordination in the growth of power, wisdom, and love. The development of power and knowledge is what the breakthroughs in science and technology bring to man. But knowledge is not in itself wisdom. Wisdom is the capacity to discern what is truly good. The development of this capacity has not yet kept pace with the growth of power. Here we face a disequilibrium capable of destroying man.

Here is the most pressing demand on the church—to produce human beings who are nurtured in a loving community of the Spirit, who both have access to the power provided by science and technology and also are able wisely to control and guide the use of these in the best interests of mankind and its future as the bearer of the image of God. A new breed of human beings have to be born who are completely at home in the world of science and technology, whose consciousness is not limited by the dogmatism and superstitions of a false scientism, and who are able to develop an open consciousness, with true wisdom and love. There is a tendency among many to decry the efforts at genetic mutation and at artificial creation of life as "tinkering with the sacred." This attitude seems to counsel a kind of complacency with the way things are. Man cannot remain stationary without becoming stagnant and deteriorating. He is meant to explore all, but he must also learn to love all and live with all in wisdom and grace. All this is part of the freedom of man.

CHAPTER VI

The Way Forward

One respects words. But words have certain limits. A reality, in order to happen, does not always first take shape in words and then take flesh. This book does not presume to show the way forward for overcoming the crisis of authority and for developing genuine human freedom at the same time. For if the essence of free humanity could be put down in words before it actually came into existence, then it would be neither free nor therefore human. For man's authentic existence has to be lived out first before it is described.

Yet words have a task—to stand by and serve, without dictating. And the following words may be taken as invitations to experimentation, not as formulae for conceptual resolution of these problems.

We need to seek liberation from the intellectual pseudomorphosis of Christianity which took place long ago. The martyr was the earliest missionary. And he was no wordmonger but a blood-spiller who spoke the powerful language of life and death. So also was the monk who followed the martyr once the persecutions came to an end. His way of life was prophetic and eschatological, and so he became by his very life and power a missionary. The monk did not peddle a pot of message, but by severe contempt of the values of a smug society he paved the way for a new world, built on discipline and self-control.

What about the layman and the laywoman who have today come into the missionary inheritance of the martyr and the monk? We clergymen have given them a lot of words. But they need to create something more vital than words in order to have an effective ministry as the new martyrs and monks of our era. They, especially the young among them, will have to show, like the martyr, the total abandonment of personal interests and, like the monk of the fourth century, should show their contempt of the values of a decadent society by creating a new one in daring and pioneering.

Problems of authority and freedom are thus problems of pioneering, not merely of conceptual clarification. The following conceptual statements are then made as suggestions to create the kind of authority and freedom that can only be lived.

THE REPLACEMENT OF THE KING BY THE SHEPHERD

This is the most dramatic insight in the Judeo-Christian tradition. Today we have seen the last of the kings. Royalty as an institution has had its day. If there still remain a few kings and sheikhs, little Duvaliers and big Francos, they belong to a bygone age.

But it would be a mistake to assume that arbitrary authority is now being replaced by "persuasive" authority. That is a comfortable luxury for bourgeois Platos and Whiteheads. What is increasingly coming into prominence is the authority of the shepherd.

There is a tendency to identify the shepherd too easily with the bishop, and to regard the sheep as very sheepish indeed. The analogy is not to be pressed at the point of the sheep. The Old Testament made much of the shepherd—a very un-Hellenic tradition.

The shepherd par excellence is God himself. Yahweh is called the shepherd of Israel.[79] In him Israel finds her security, protection, providence, and affectionate care. In fact, Yahweh is Israel's shepherd-king. He does appoint another shepherd in his place to look after the people. Moses was the first such shepherd. When Moses was getting too aged to feed the sheep on behalf of Yahweh, he said to the Lord:

> May Yahweh the Lord of the spirits of all flesh appoint a man over the community, who shall lead them in going out and coming in, who will take them out and bring them in, lest the community of Yahweh become like a flock for which there is no shepherd. (Num. 27:16–17.)

Joshua becomes thus the shepherd of Israel. Shepherd or pastor in the Old Testament certainly does not mean priest; it means, rather, the civil ruler. Ezekiel's prophecies against the shepherds of Israel (ch. 34:2 ff.) are directed against her civil rulers. What are the charges against them?

> Thus says Adonai Yahweh
> Hoi, shepherds of Israel
> Who have been tending your own selves
> Should not shepherds tend the sheep?
> You eat the fat, you put on the wool,
> You slaughter the fatlings, but the sheep you do not tend.
> You have not strengthened the weak
> You have not healed the sick
> You have not bound up the crippled
> You have not brought back the strayed
> You have not sought the lost ones
> With brute force and harshness you have ruled them
> So they were scattered
> And became a prey for all wild beasts.

Here we see clearly that Israel went wrong in regarding law and order rather than welfare as the primary duty of the state.

Ezekiel goes on to say that the sheep themselves have become unjust because of the lack of good government.

> Thus says the Lord GOD to them [the flock]: "Behold, I, I myself will judge between the fat sheep and the lean sheep. Because you push with side and shoulder, and thrust at all the weak with your horns, till you have scattered them abroad, I will save my flock, they shall no longer be a prey; and I will judge between sheep and sheep. And I will set up over them one shepherd, my servant David, and he shall feed them: he shall feed them and be their shepherd. And I, the LORD, will be their God, and my servant David shall be prince among them; I, the LORD, have spoken." (Ezek. 34:20–24.)

The messianic expectation in Israel was thus closely connected with waiting for the "Good Shepherd" who not only will feed his flock but will also protect the weak sheep against the fat and mighty within the flock. In the tenth chapter of the Fourth Gospel, Jesus claims to be the Messiah as Good Shepherd.

The qualities of the good shepherd in John, ch. 10, go far beyond the tasks of the welfare state, while including welfare. There is warm personal relation between the ruled and the rulers. (He calls his own sheep by name, and they follow.) The good shepherd finds pasture for the sheep, and defends them against wolves to the point of self-sacrifice.

It is at the moment impossible to conceive a governmental structure that will embody all these principles. But our task is to establish at least experimental communities where the shepherdly pattern of rule replaces that of arbitrary authority.

The authority of the devoted and self-sacrificing leader is still a reality even in this democratic age. The way forward to the healing of humanity lies primarily through the recovery of this type of authority in communities, and eventually in the whole world.

THE DE-CEREBRATION OF FAITH AND KNOWLEDGE

Quite apart from the pseudomorphosis of Christianity or perhaps as a remote consequence of it, the Western mind has preoccupied itself with the *forms* of knowledge, and not with wisdom. Perhaps it was a quest for certainty. Only by knowing how we know can we know how certain that knowledge is.

There were only two forms of knowing—through the senses, or through the mind. The first approach leads to empiricism in epistemology; the second to rationalism. In both, true being becomes identified with the forms of knowledge—either the state of consciousness or the forms of cognition. When this identification raises unanswerable questions about the nature of the "thing-in-itself," we deny ontology and metaphysics altogether, and retreat to a functionalist-existentialist fortress. There too we are uncomfortable. And we make sorties into tactile knowledge—body contacts, experimental investigations, and so on; or else we escape into the pure inner world which can be created by drugs or psychedelics.

Man's freedom demands that we move out of this fortress. Modern youth is impatient with the functionalism of the traditional technological civilization.

In the last century Vladimir Soloviev wrote about the dangers of cerebration. First one hypostatizes abstract predicates; then one doubts their reality. The next stage is to question the reality of all being except one's own consciousness. But trying to get hold of the true being of beings with our rational minds is like seeking to catch the waterfall in a sieve. For, as Nyssa has shown, the true being of all that exists is nothing less than the dynamic will of God. And we cannot grasp that will in our concepts.

The major weakness of the Christian faith has been the attempt to conceptualize faith, to formulate it, and to hold it in words. But faith is a relation to the being and will of God. It cannot be reduced to words and concepts which we can control. Words can only stand by and serve. Man must come to terms with reality in the act of worship. There words have a role to play, but a quite limited role. Cerebration is part of celebration, but cannot replace it. The de-cerebration of faith and knowledge can come only in acts of worship which go beyond the verbal and the conceptual. Worship must thus involve the use of the whole body, of things and actions, of emotion and will, and of trans-conceptual expressions of aspiration and exultation.

The liturgy of the Eucharist has to be recovered in all its original completeness—the mind (conscious and unconscious), the will, the emotions, the body, the senses, all being equally involved. The corporateness of humanity, living and departed, history, present, and future—these have to be experienced in worship. The kingdom as that which transcends and comprehends the spatio-temporal has to be tasted in worship. Only thus can man move toward the fullness of freedom.

Our "new" forms of worship remain banal in their verbality, in their lack of appeal to the body and the will, in their self-conscious individualism, in their imprisonment in the concerns of the immediate present. A richer and fuller worship is the *sine qua non* for holding the Christian faith alive and moving toward freedom.

A New Awareness of a Universal Tradition

The West, much more than the East, has acquired a very negative attitude toward tradition and the past. Tradition is so full of errors and crimes that it is easier to forget the past and set one's sights on the future. This is particularly so for the church, because a study of the past reveals so many arrogant false claims, so much imposition of blatant error on others by force, so much suppression of freedom, so much silly dogmatism.

And yet the recovery of an authentic tradition, with a conscious acknowledgment of past errors, seems absolutely necessary both for the recovery of credibility and for a dynamic approach to the future. Perhaps it is unsettling to be aware of one's errors in the past, for then one may become less cocksure about the future. Yet without mitigating that cocksureness, we may be repeating the history of false claims even in the future. By becoming less cocksure, the West may be unable to hold its position of leadership, but it may in that process open itself more to unsuspected dimensions of truth.

It should be possible for the West to find a *via media* between an absolutely self-confident messianism and a totally self-abdicating, hand-wringing, withdrawal. That can be done by honest self-evaluation and self-awareness with humility and openness toward other civilizations and cultures. That is what true tradition is—an awareness of both what is good and what is bad in one's own racial-cultural past—not a false glorification or total condemnation of it.

The whole of humanity needs a common tradition, one that belongs to the whole of mankind because tradition now acts divisively. Each race and sect and nation and linguistic group seeks to defend its own tradition over against others. The full freedom of man demands that we unite our traditions and hold the whole thing, with all its successes and failures, as our common heritage. No true vision of the future of humanity is possible without the acknowledgment of the past of humanity as belonging to all of us together. A major battle to be won for the freedom of man is the creation of a common human history which makes all human beings capable of saying "we" in terms of that common history. No particular tradition can be fully trusted, except in the context of an openness to the sum total of human experience, culture, and wisdom.

The question of authority here receives a new perspective. Here I am, an Indian, a member of an Eastern Orthodox church, trained in the Western system of education. I inherit thus three traditions—the cultural-spiritual heritage of India, the religious-spiritual heritage of Eastern Christianity, and the conceptual formation of Western civilization. If I had to choose one of these to the exclusion of the two others, I would have been that much impoverished. How do I then find my way? Can I first make a comparative study of two or three religious traditions and then choose one of them on the basis of externally testable superiority? Hardly—the Hindu and Buddhist religions belong to my cultural heritage. Hinduism has its own scriptures as has Christianity. Hindu seers and thinkers claim with at least as much sincerity as Christian theologians and clergymen that their scriptures are uniquely authoritative and convey a special revelation from God unavailable through ordinary human thought and experience.

Faced with two rival and exclusive claims to divine revelation, how do I choose? What external criteria can help me decide? I do not think there is a valid answer to that question. A number of predilections and circumstances have led me to a choice—specifically for Eastern Christianity as my primary commitment.

But precisely because I hold a whole human experience as my heritage, I cannot be exclusive in my adherence to Eastern Christianity. I have learned much by being open to both Western Christianity and Hinduism, as well as to Judaism, Islam, Buddhism, secular humanism, and Marxism. All these belong to my tradition. But I cannot trust my own judgment as a criterion. So I do not remain in a floating relation to all my heritage, but have consciously chosen one limited heritage, from which to receive my perspective on other parts of my heritage. This I do by belonging to a community and accepting its heritage as a perspective-granting criterion for evaluation and living out other aspects of my heritage.

I cannot claim any neutral authority for my choice. My own experience confirms that I have made the right choice. But then I know others who have made a different choice in similar circumstances and I cannot claim that their experience gives them no confirmation of their choice. In other words, choices are made, not on the basis of an objective external authority, but rather on the basis of a set of predilections and circumstances. It seems idle to claim an objective criterion on the basis of which anyone can choose between the Christian Bible and the Hindu scriptures. If such criteria are offered, they are usually derived from the tradition that one has already chosen.

The adherence to a particular tradition and a religious community is thus a risk for which we have to accept responsibility. No one can really remain a "gliding philosopher" for all his life without serious disintegration of personality. Commitment to one particular tradition makes it easier to be open to the wealth of all traditions. Genuine freedom is not lost by such commitment. On the contrary, one begins to feel free to deal with all the rich variety only when one is secure within one tradition. Those without such security become either incredibly fanatic, or rather sadly eclectic and therefore unfree.

The authority we thus accept is primarily that of God as he reveals himself in the life of a community. The scriptures of that community bear witness to that experience of the community with God. The experience of the community is primary; the experience of individuals in that community is secondary. The scriptures bear witness to both; but the scriptures themselves cannot be understood or evaluated without membership in the community and participation in its experience. Hence the impossibility of objective comparative study of the various religions by looking at their scriptures.

The scriptures are by no means exhaustive of the experience of the community. They are only a standard by which that wealth of experience can be measured and understood. It is the collective mind of the community that stores the experience. The scriptures are a mnemonic device for the community, a criterion by which the community can itself check and correct its memory. Authority for faith and conduct thus is not in the scriptures. It is in the life of the community. But it is a very flexible and open kind of authority, to be corrected by the sum total of experience, by openness to reality wherever it manifests itself, and by growth in maturity of understanding and judgment.

That is why tradition always has to have an eschatological dimension and orientation. Tradition is not backward-looking. It appropriates the past in order to be more adequately open to the future. Tradition is always a reaching forward to direct vision, to unmediated knowledge, and to the consummation of love. Loyalty to tradition without openness to present reality and expectant yearning for the future can be stifling and destructive of human freedom. But an openness to the future without an awareness of the past is bound to be superficial and therefore enslaving. The community of the spirit lives out of the past toward the future in the present. There freedom grows, for the spirit is freedom.

THE DISCIPLINED COMMUNITY

True growth of freedom demands a disciplined community. Belonging to a large church or religious group does not provide one with all that is necessary for human growth. The family is the primary small community for all human beings. It is there that the basic human elements of conscience, self-control, and discipline as well as the capacity for love are acquired. The family provides the child first with the security of love which makes creative spontaneity possible. Where the child does not experience this security and love, it will be restless and anxious, unable to enter into relationships with anyone, threatened by the very encounter with others.

It is also in the family that conscience and self-control are acquired. First the parent acts as monitor for the child in many matters of conduct including toilet and feeding habits, which the child does quite mechanically in the early stages. Slowly the child gets the notion of right and wrong, and begins to exercise self-control in toilet and feeding habits as well as later in more complex moral decisions.

The school, the church, the club, the professional group—
all these communities teach more and more habits of self-
regulation and principles of conscience to the adolescent and
the adult. But today the need seems to be for a community
that, by providing a framework, can help man to acquire
genuine internal and external freedom in a more systematic
and consciously directed way than can these randomly run
institutions of society.

Mere repression of passions cannot give us victory over our
passions, we have learned to our cost in the last century.
Today there is a reaction against repressive moral codes as
destructive of genuine freedom. Herbert Marcuse reminds us
that our whole civilization suffers from our repressive tendencies which generate acquisitiveness and aggressiveness.
Marcuse criticizes Freud for asserting that civilization can be
built only by the methodical inhibition of the primary instincts
—the inhibition of sexuality and the repression of the destructive instinct. It is through these two basic repressions that
individual and social morality is born, according to Freud.
And that morality is the basis and dynamo of our civilization.

Marcuse would argue that this civilization develops com-
pensatory aggressiveness and acquisitiveness, precisely because of such repression.[80] Knowledge and work become
oriented toward struggle, conquest, and domination of one's
environment. Objective reality is resistance, and action and
knowledge are ways of overcoming the resistance. The ego
itself thus becomes oriented toward aggressive domination. In
this overemphasis of the male principle of aggressive domination, the complementary female principle of receptivity and
gratification are overlooked and frustrated. Our present revolt
against arbitrary authority may be seen partly as a revolt
against the structure of society which is based on the principle
that the strong man establishes his ego by aggressively dominating the other and making the other an adjunct of one's own
ego.

Marcuse would also argue for the possibility of a civilization in which ego-formation itself takes a different pattern—"a non-repressive civilization" coming out of a "non-repressive development of the libido under the conditions of mature civilization." [81] The strict adherence to the "reality principle," on which modern Western civilization is built, has, however, not completely eliminated the other aspect, the "pleasure principle" which continues to function, unrepressed, in human fantasy. Out of this fantasy is born art, which is a feeble and largely ineffective critique of the reality principle. But fantasy, imagination, says Carl Jung, and Marcuse agrees, is the matrix of all future human possibility. Fantasy both recaptures the ancient past and freely creates the distant future. The reality principle intervenes to deride imagination's creations of the future as utopian. Yet fantasy continues to daydream.

Marcuse argues, somewhat convincingly, for elimination of at least the "surplus repression" now used for aggressive domination, and thus for achieving a balanced synthesis between the reality and the pleasure principles. He thinks this can be done when mankind is no longer organized for labor, but labor is automated and organized for mankind.

This excursus into the complicated theories of Marcuse was necessitated by our demand for a fresh form of discipline for a community—not authoritarian and repressive, not based purely on the "performance" or "reality" principle. Marcuse would agree with most of us that we need to increase our production in order to assure abundance for all. But productivity itself need not enslave man and make him adjunct to the machine. Production, when fully automated, can become play.

Can we conceive a disciplined community where work is play, where the reality principle and pleasure principle are mutually reconciled, where repression is released into sublimated expression, where authority is mutual and shepherdly, where freedom flourishes? Perhaps not as easily as Marcuse proposes. He argues primarily for a "non-repressive sublimation" of sexuality as the first stage toward a new civilization. This would also mean a decentralization of sexuality from the domination of genital contact to a more polymorphous enjoyment. He thinks also that work itself, when no longer based on repression, can be turned to libidinous pleasure. He thus argues for a "non-repressive libidinous civilization." There is no need to wonder why Marcuse becomes the pet prophet of the younger generation. They too sometimes feel that the culture of repressive restraint unnecessarily denies them the simple pleasures of sexuality. They see no rational ground for the Victorian system of morality still so widely professed.

But in the disciplined community whose purpose is to enhance and nurture human freedom, what sort of a discipline do we propose? Of course, the pattern of such a community can emerge only through direct experimentation. And principles such as those enunciated by Marcuse should be examined carefully before we experiment with them.

We can agree with Marcuse at least about the stifling and distorting effects of excessive repression. And he himself often claims that it is only "superfluous repression" that he is opposing. Strangely enough the whole development in the field of clinical psychology is away from excessive permissiveness and "non-directiveness." It is becoming clinically clear that man requires external restraint and direction in order to grow into full maturity. The total neutrality and noninterference of the analyst is now understood to be derived from the values of a bourgeois-liberal culture. On the other hand the simple monastic rules of poverty, chastity, and obedience are inadequate for the discipline of the new community of freedom.

There should be a balance, though not a strict parity, between the following elements in the discipline of the Christian community that we have in mind:

1. Social control and personal initiative
2. Work and play, drudgery and the dance
3. Productive labor and relaxed leisure

4. Corporate and personal prayer and worship on the one hand, and humor on the other
5. Study and artistic creativity
6. Separation from society and direct involvement in it
7. Fasting and feasting
8. Mutual acceptance and honest criticism

Experimental communities will have to question the accepted norms of society by practicing values that are freely and wisely chosen by it. International and interracial communities, with a minimum of commitment of at least three years' membership and a core of people committed for life to each other, are the best. Such communities will certainly want to question both the productivity principle and the reality principle of our civilization. They would not shirk work, but will seek to make work itself a joyous thing. They will learn strict and joyful repression of the instinctual drives in man—not for the sake of productivity, nor for domination of others, but for control of oneself, without which there is no freedom. They will at the same time also be able to enjoy food and drink and the simple pleasures of life on occasion, without a sense of guilt. They will probably have a "leader," possibly on a rotation system. They will not all be of the same age or sex. Ideally, there could be celibate communities and married communities within one complex.

As for sexual morality, especially in Western societies where the social relations between the sexes have become more evolved, it should be possible for the celibates as well as the married couples and their children to form a free and dignified society of human beings where mutual respect and love can enable each to sublimate his or her drive to exploit each other sexually. This sublimation need not be in terms of a "genito-fugal" direction of sexuality into polymorphous or pansomatic expressions. It could take the much more creative form of hard toil, personal sacrifice for the poor and the oppressed, profound worship and prayer accompanied by fasting and, above all, love. Love for children, love for the weak and the exploited, compassion for those who are the oppressors and exploiters—all these are methods of sublimation which have stood the test of time.

It is as much a mistake to see human sexuality as a merely biological matter, as to ignore its biological aspects. Man is an animal, but certainly he is much more than an animal. Human sexuality has of course several elements common to all animals; but its essence goes deep into the social and personal roots of man. The ancient Christian tendency to regard the sexual relationship as sinful is no doubt a fundamental error. But perhaps it could be phenomenologically demonstrated that human sin produces at least as many complications in the sexual relationship as almost in any other realm of human existence.

The very fact that the Christian church itself has been quite shy[82] about discussing sexuality seems instructive. Sixteenth-century Puritanism must have inherited this shyness from an earlier tradition. But the shyness is itself not without meaning. The sex drive is so much in the center of our consciousness that there is no need to exacerbate it further by conscious discussion or description. Fallen man is one of the most oversexed of animals.

Freud was fundamentally right in affirming that culture is the consequence of repressed sexuality. Perhaps Freud himself was obsessed with the idea of repression, as there is good reason to believe. As Norman Brown put it, "In the . . . Freudian perspective, the essence of society is repression of the individual, and the essence of the individual is repression of himself." [83] And what is repression? "The essence of repression lies simply in the function of rejecting or keeping something out of consciousness." [84] Brown reinterprets these words to mean "the refusal of the human being to recognize the realities of his human nature."

And as usual, Brown is right, but in a perverted way. The point is that man is the animal who is required to refuse to accept the reality of his being as given, and is put under pressure to make himself into something else than his given reality. Man cannot become man if he simply accepts himself as he is. Mere acceptance may mean refusal to change. We can see this from our own use of language. Take the word "humanization." Mankind has to be "humanized." This obviously means that man is not human yet. I doubt if the cows talk about "bovinization" or the cats about "felinization." If man accepts himself as he is, he ceases to be man.

Repression is only a distorted symbol of three fundamental realities in the existence of man. First, man is the animal who is under pressure of "becoming," and is unable to escape this pressure. If he does not become what he ought to be, he will become what he ought not to be, but he is not allowed to remain what he is or appears to be. Second, man has to attain freedom, and this can be achieved only by gaining mastery over one's consciousness itself. The mind itself has to be brought under control. Repression is the distorted expression of a human characteristic, namely, the pressure to be master of one's own thoughts, feelings, desires, and drives. If, as Freud says, the essence of man is in willing or desiring, then man is not free until he is liberated from compulsive desires which make him do or desire what he does not freely choose, obedient even to desires he really detests. Third, the fact that there are desires that we want to repress, and that we are afraid even to acknowledge the existence of, points to something fundamentally wrong in human nature as it is given. It is not simply that there is a conflict between the pleasure principle and the reality principle. Both principles belong to the essence of man. Man is meant to rejoice (pleasure) in the truth (reality). Only attempts prematurely to settle down to the enjoyment of reality before we have become mature enough to do so are called in question. Love and truth are the ultimates. But so long as we are ourselves untruth, we cannot truly love or love the truth. Human nature remains a task to be achieved.

Sexual drives and desires of aggression (including murder) are the ones most subject to repression. And these two types of desires are linked together. They are perverted manifestations of a healthy drive in man to rejoice in love, and to be master of the universe. The drive for joy in love becomes distorted as sexual exploitation of others, and the drive for mastery becomes corrupted into the desire to attack and destroy the other who does not accept my mastery over him or her. Sexuality and aggression thus relate to an inner world and a pattern of relationships which turbulently revolt against the control of man and which man is under pressure to bring under control. True freedom demands that man be in control of the "inner" world in our consciousness, and the "outer" world of other beings in time and space. An excess of the sexual drive is thus a challenge to the freedom of man, an indicator that his consciousness is not within control.

Both celibacy as a life vocation and temporary celibacy for married couples during certain days of the week and seasons of the year (fasts or Lent) are instituted by the church in order to assist man, whether celibate or married, to achieve mastery over the inner world of consciousness. Is this not tantamount to saying that repression is good and that the Victorian ideal (not always practiced) is also the Christian ideal? Certainly not. The plea is not for repression, but for freedom in the consciousness. Man is not meant to be a plaything of the sexual urge, or even of the urge to eat and drink, though none of these urges are wrong or sinful in themselves. The principle is the Pauline one: "Everything is permissible but not everything is appropriate. Everything is possible, but not everything helps to build up. Don't, however, decide questions of ethics in an individual context, but with full awareness of the consequence of your actions for others." (I Cor. 10:23–24, paraphrase.)

Much of the dynamic of early Christianity came from a rigorous sexual ethic coupled with a deep life of prayer. Even the dynamic of British imperialism in the nineteenth century was not unconnected with a Victorian sexual ethic. The dis-integration of the Roman Empire was also not unconnected with a dissolute sexual ethic. Our need today is to find non-repressive ways of channeling sexual energy (libido) into creative endeavors. Only revolutionary or enthusiastic move-ments can consume that energy in a creative manner. A passion for justice can consume much of this bottled-up sexual energy. Mere indiscriminate indulgence of the sexual drive simply brings us under greater enslavement to something over which we have less and less control.

A new sexual ethic, in order to be Christian, cannot just be a "permissive" one. It has to be a "creative" one in which the mind, the emotions, the will, and the body are aflame with the fire of the kingdom of God, combining worship and the struggle for justice in one impassioned endeavor. Only that way can the consciousness be cleared up and brought under control again. And then, within the marriage bond of com-mitted love, sex can be enjoyed with relish and without guilt. Freud himself spoke about sublimation as a creative way of utilizing excessive libidinal energy. Repression, by concen-trating directly on the drives and seeking to inhibit them, makes their reaction more furious, even if furtive. The sexual drives of many monks and celibates, when directly repressed, become compulsively neurotic traits of character just as ob-jectionable as licentious sexual activity.

Sublimation demands not a placid state of inactivity, but a continuous passion for God and fellowmen, pouring itself out in worship or the love of God and service or the love of man. One of these two by itself cannot achieve perfect sublimation. This is the reason why monks and priests become neurotic when they neglect the love of fellowmen and the needs of people in the world. But similarly, activists also become neurotic when their inner being is not continuously refreshed by the love of God.

The "new morality," which simply seeks to replace sexual repression by sexual expression, is bound to be disillusioning, as many young people have already begun to find out. But when libidinal energy is channeled into community and personal worship (with strong emphasis on adoration and intercession) and loving and compassionate service to human beings (mere political activity to change structures will not suffice), then a new level of human freedom can be experienced. There is thus a new opportunity for genuine freedom in the sexual revolution, but certainly not in the direction of the "new morality."

Equally ludicrous is the "gay revolution" about which one does not speak here without sympathy and fellow feeling. One is able, however, to affirm that most forms of homosexuality can be overcome if a sufficient discipline of sublimation is applied in the early stages. The callous kind of ostracism with which society now faces the homosexual has no full justification. But encouraging the homosexual to practice his homosexuality in a legitimate manner by legalizing "gay marriages" seems only an invitation to calamity. Such relationships are essentially ephemeral, and separation, when it comes, often leads to violent and aggressive fits of temper. People only destroy themselves by indulging themselves homosexually. Once again the only sane advice to be given to those in the early stages of homosexuality is either to get married to someone of the opposite sex who could reactivate the latent capacity for heterosexuality in the individual, and in any case, whether married or unmarried, to find channels for worship and service wherein to sublimate the excess libidinal energy. The way that is being popularly proposed today can lead only to enslavement and misery. The way to freedom here also lies, not in repression, but in disciplined sublimation.

The Christian affirmation that in heaven there is neither marriage nor birth, and therefore no sexuality in our sense, deserves more consideration by theologians. But mutuality and interpenetration in love belong in the essence of heaven. The problem with repression of sex is that it is often also repression of love. Love is ultimate reality, both in heaven and on earth. Sex at the service of love can take the form of marriage or celibacy, but in both adoring worship and loving service are the means to transfigure sex into an expression of freedom, which is the invariable concomitant of true love.

Nonrepressive sublimation of the sex instinct *is* possible. In fact, there can be no genuine growth into freedom without overcoming the instinctual drives of the libido. Trouble comes when that self-control becomes so obsessive as to make one forget the outside world of other human beings toward whom all our emotional energy has to be directed in love and compassion.

The Christian faith teaches that a tensionless existence is not given to Christians on this earth. The proposed community will not be a paradise on earth without any tensions or failures and explosions. Yet the renewal of society does not seem possible without experimental communities of this type, which create new patterns of sane human existence and create sane and authentic human personalities.

Discipline externally provided and freely interiorized is an essential component of human freedom. All the student and youth protest of our time is crying out for channels of creativity. Disciplined communities organized with imaginative freedom seem to be capable of providing such channels. It is important, however, to guard against the tyranny of structures. The structures are created by us for our training. They are to be discarded as early as possible and new ones assumed for more intensive training of human freedom and creativity. If, on the other hand, we absolutize any structure or pattern of community, we may soon be enslaved by it and lose the freedom we thought we had gained.

The growth of freedom calls for eternal vigilance. In fact, this vigilance is the true Christian eschatological attitude. We are never allowed to settle down on earth or go to sleep. "Watch!" That is what Christ demands of his disciples.

The creation of several experimental communities in several places and diverse circumstances, with some measure of com-

munity among the small communities, may be part of our way
forward. All such communities will be directly oriented to the
problems of humanity and not simply inward-looking. Yet
even in their engagement in the affairs of the world, they will
be capable of the disengagement of worship in the joy of
freedom, where they can close the portals of history and enter
into the *eschaton* where that history is already fulfilled.

Conclusion

We began this inquiry into the dialectic between authority and freedom with an evaluation of several movements in our time. It was suggested that most of these were attempts to solve the issues on an intellectual plane first. Some intellectual misapprehensions were then discussed, and it was pointed out that ultimately the solutions have to be worked out in experimental communities.

At this stage we mean primarily Christian ecumenical communities. Not that non-Christians will not be able to experiment successfully. If they succeed, we should learn from them. But as Christians we have a special responsibility to pioneer in experimental community living. For that is what it means to be the light of the world.

But such communities cannot at the moment be composed predominantly of white Westerners. We might need to include Christians from other lands and cultures, who bring with them a different spirituality. Perhaps since most non-Western Christians have acquired a semi-Western spirituality, it may be necessary to include Muslims, Jews, Hindus, Buddhists, and humanists who bring a non-Western element into the Christian community. One has seen too often how Christians who constantly talk of de-Westernization of Christianity are the least capable of themselves being de-Westernized.

Such a community cannot create authentic human freedom without the aid of structures. Unstructured life cannot produce freedom, *pace* Marcuse. But structure itself has to be discardable, and one has to be fully vigilant not to be enslaved by it. A structure is something which we must create in order to train ourselves. But we must also be capable of destroying what we create when it becomes a threat to us.

There is a general kind of form for this structure which is suggested by the tradition of the church. This is where authority comes in—to suggest forms for structures, and thus to keep us within the structures. The Scriptures, the Eucharist, the fathers of the church, the liturgical year prescribed by the church, the fasts and offices proposed by the church, the decisions of the Councils—all these are raw materials for building structures of authentic existence. Their authority should never become tyrannical. But without these, we may be experimenting in ways destructive of true freedom and authentic humanity.

There is no need to bewail the breakdown of authority in our time. That is the only way we can be made to understand and accept authority as a form for freedom. Finally, there is no necessary conflict between freedom and structure. Authority is only an aspect of structure. Such authority can take any of the forms described in the second chapter. But all of them are only protective frames for the growth of freedom. Freedom should outgrow all structures. For the full-grown saint, neither the Scriptures nor the tradition were any longer necessary. But during his period of growth to sainthood they were necessary. He might have made shipwreck of his life if he had experimented entirely on his own.

Authority, whether it be of a book, of a spiritual superior, or of the community, belongs to the early stages of the growth of human freedom. We cannot easily dispense with them and expect man to grow to the fullness of his freedom. Even young people who are most in revolt have a nostalgia for authentic authority and they need this authority. Whether in the church, or in education, this new type of self-authenticating, self-effacing, self-sacrificing authority which comes from the combination of disciplined power, love, and wisdom, alone can show the way forward. But in the end, all authority can be discarded. It is like the wooden frame necessary for making reinforced concrete. Without that frame the concrete cannot take the desired shape. But the frame itself has no value once the concrete has solidified and cured beyond danger of distortion.

Man is born to be king. His vocation ultimately is to rule, not to be ruled. He is in the image of God. But he must grow to that image in freedom, i.e., by developing freedom through wise use of the structures of authority. The structures should, however, never be allowed to enslave him, or distort love and justice in the community.

Because man is born to be king, government is man's business, and the business of all men. That is why ultimately no man should be subject to the authority of another. All men should play their part in governing or controlling society and its common activities. The man who was born to be king is everyman, or rather the whole of mankind. There is no true freedom for man until the whole of mankind becomes liberated and is able to rule. The ultimate freedom of man in history would be when all have become free and mature, needing no authority, all committed totally to the welfare of mankind, and all using their disciplined power, love, and wisdom for the whole of mankind.

There is no stopping place short of that. That end, however, like the horizon, will constantly keep receding. Man is a quest for freedom, freedom that goes on questing throughout history, for He who was truly free entered that history two thousand years ago and has started a work which he will also bring to completion.

The end itself is beyond history. It is trans-temporal. That means it is not just the last generation that will see the end. We are moving on to the trans-temporal beyond the veil. There freedom takes new shapes and beckons to new horizons of fulfillment. The march of freedom is ceaseless for it is the march toward the being of him who created the world in freedom, who dwells in unapproachable light, who is Freedom.

Notes

1. Karl Jaspers, *Man in the Modern Age*, tr. by Eden and Cedar Paul (Doubleday & Company, Inc., Anchor Books, 1957), p. 152.

2. Carl Friedrich von Weizsäcker, *The Relevance of Science: Creation and Cosmogony* (London: Collins, 1964).

3. *Ibid.*, p. 125.

4. *Ibid.*, p. 146.

5. *x* can be anywhere from 10 to 30.

6. *Ibid.*, p. 126.

7. *Ibid.*, p. 178.

8. *Ibid.*, p. 12.

9. Vol. XII (Jan., 1878), pp. 286–302. Quoted in Morton White (ed.), *The Age of Analysis* (New American Library, Inc., Mentor Books, 1958), pp. 141–142.

10. Werner Brock in his introduction to Martin Heidegger, *Existence and Being* (Henry Regnery Company, Gateway Paperbacks, 1949), p. 166.

11. W. R. Miller, ed., *The New Christianity* (Dell Publishing Co., Inc., Delta Books, 1967).

12. William Blake, "The Everlasting Gospel," cited in Miller, *op. cit.*, p. 28.

13. Thomas J. J. Altizer, *The Gospel of Christian Atheism* (The Westminster Press, 1966), p. 93.

14. Friedrich Nietzsche, *The Antichrist*, Sect. 18. From Walter Kaufmann (tr.), *The Portable Nietzsche* (The Viking Press, Inc., 1954).

15. Friedrich Nietzsche, *The Joyful Wisdom*, tr. by Thomas Common, in Friedrich Nietzsche, *Complete Works*, Vol. X, ed. by Oscar Levy (Edinburgh: T. N. Foulis, 1910).

16. See Dietrich Ritschl, *Memory and Hope: An Inquiry Concerning the Presence of Christ* (The Macmillan Company, 1968).

17. Leslie Dewart, *The Future of Belief: Theism in a World Come of Age* (Herder and Herder, 1966).

18. Leslie Dewart, "God and the Supernatural," *Commonweal*, Feb. 10, 1967. Reprinted in *New Theology No. 5*, ed. by Martin E. Marty and Dean G. Peerman (The Macmillan Company, 1968), p. 152.

19. *Ibid.*, p. 155.

20. See Ernst Bloch's later book, *Philosophische Grundfragen zur Ontologie des Noch-Nicht-Seins* (Frankfurt: Suhrkamp Verlag, 1961).

21. A very useful collection of these and other early MSS. has been edited and translated by Lloyd D. Easton and Kurt H. Guddat: *Writings of the Young Marx on Philosophy and Society* (Doubleday & Company, Inc., Anchor Books, 1967).

22. Erich Fromm (ed.), *Socialist Humanism: An International Symposium* (Doubleday & Company, Inc., Anchor Books, 1966).

23. "The Son of man has authority (*exousia*) on earth to forgive sins . . ." (Matt. 9:6). "All authority (*exousia*) in heaven and on earth has been given to me. Go therefore . . . ." (Matt. 28:18.)

24. See, e.g., *Dialogues of Alfred North Whitehead*, as recorded by Lucien Price (Little, Brown and Company, 1954); or Alfred North Whitehead, *Adventures of Ideas* (New American Library, Inc., Mentor Books, 1955).

25. Martin Buber, "On the Suspension of the Ethical," essay in his *Eclipse of God* (Harper & Brothers, 1957), pp. 155 ff.

26. *Oratio in sanctum baptisma*, 40:45, in J. P. Migne (ed.),

Patrologiae cursus completus: Series Graeca (Paris, 1857–66), Vol. 36, p. 424 A. (Also referred to as *Patrologia Graeca,* this work will be cited hereafter as PG.)

27. The Great Catechism, V, in Philip Schaff and Henry Wace (eds.), *The Select Library of the Nicene and Post-Nicene Fathers of the Christian Church,* 2d Series (New York, 1890–1900), Vol. V, p. 479. (Cited hereafter as NPNF 2 ser.)

28. See *Retractationes,* I:ix.

29. Rom. 5:12—Sin entered the world.

30. Rom. 6:11 ff.

31. Sermons, CCLXIV:4.

32. *In Ps.,* CIX:5.

33. *In Ps.,* CXXXVI:3, 4 (NPNF 2 ser. V. 269).

34. *De genesi ad litteram,* VIII:xii:25, 27. (NPNF 2 ser. V. 306–307).

35. *In Joan. Evang.,* XXIII (NPNF 2 ser. V. 18).

36. Barbara Ward, *Faith and Freedom* (W. W. Norton & Company, Inc., 1954), p. 282.

37. See Irenaeus, Against Heresies, Bk. III:2 ff.

38. Hans Jonas, *The Gnostic Religion,* 2d ed. (Beacon Press, Inc., 1963), p. 32.

39. Origen, *On First Principles,* tr. by G. W. Butterworth (Harper & Row, Publishers, 1966), p. 2.

40. *Ibid.,* p. 166 (III: 6).

41. First Theological Oration, III (NPNF 2 ser. VII. 285).

42. See Titus 2:1, 2, 8.

43. St. Basil, *The Letters,* tr. by Roy J. Deferrari (G. P. Putnam's Sons, The Loeb Classical Library, 1926), Vol. I, p. 93.

44. Plato in *Timaeus,* 28 E.

45. Second Theological Oration, IV (PG 36, Oratio XXVIII).

46. *Ibid.,* XVII. (See NPNF 2 ser. VII. 294).

47. Second Theological Oration, X (PG 36, Oratio XXVIII).

48. Ch. III. (NPNF 2 ser. V. 477).

49. Werner Jaeger, *Two Rediscovered Works of Ancient Christian Literature: Gregory of Nyssa and Macarius* (Leiden: E. J. Brill, 1954); Werner Jaeger *et al., Gregorii Nysseni opera ascetica* (Leiden: E. J. Brill, 1952).

50. Hans von Balthasar, *Présence et Pensée, Essai sur la Philosophie Religieuse de Grégoire de Nysse* (Paris: Gabriel Beauchesne, 1942).

51. *Eleutheros, adespotos,* and *autokratēs.* See PG 44:184 B, 45:101 D, 46:524 A.

52. *Ibid.,* 45:609 B.

53. *Ibid.,* 45:32 C, D.

54. See the vibrant criticism of Origen's Hellenism by an Eastern Orthodox scholar of the present day in Vladimir Lossky, *The Mystical Theology of the Eastern Church* (London: James Clarke & Company, Ltd., 1957), p. 32.

55. NPNF 2 ser. V. 441 B. PG 46:60 A. One of the remarkable capacities of the Cappadocians in general was to use literal interpretations where the Scriptures clearly meant that, and at the same time to demythologize concepts like creation, fall, heaven, hell, etc.

56. The Great Catechism, I (NPNF 2 ser. V. 476 A).

57. *Ibid.*

58. On the Soul and the Resurrection (NPNF 2 ser. V. 458 B, A).

59. PG 44:1137 B.

60. PG 44:1272 C.

61. Jerome Gaith, *La Conception de la Liberté chez Grégoire de Nysse* (Paris, 1953), p. 37.

62. Cf. Heidegger's questions about the being of beings and Sartre's remarks about nonbeing oozing out of every being.

63. From the conclusion of the seventh homily on Ecclesiastes (PG 46:729–732). This translation has been made from the French of Roger Leys, *L'Image de Dieu chez Saint Grégoire de Nysse* (Paris: Desclée de Brouwer, 1951).

64. *Contra Eunomium,* 1:373.

65. The Great Catechism, XXXII (NPNF 2 ser. V. 499).

66. The Great Catechism, XXXVII (NPNF 2 ser. V. 504 ff.).

67. The Great Catechism, XL (NPNF 2 ser. V. 507–508).

68. On the Making of Man, XVI, 16, 17 (NPNF 2 ser. V. 406).

69. Hans von Balthasar has a slightly different explanation

of Gregory's view of the fullness of humanity: "Human nature as a spiritual entity is a concrete universal in which innumerable individuals participate, the one being unthinkable without the other, all ideas being also at the same time entelechy." Quoted in Leys, *op. cit.*, p. 84.

70. PG 44:192 B.

71. NPNF 2 ser. V. 390.

72. *Ibid.*, pp. 393–395.

73. On the Soul and the Resurrection (NPNF 2 ser. V. 433).

74. On the Making of Man, VIII, 5 (NPNF 2 ser. V. 393–394).

75. *Rheinische Zeitung*, July, 1842. See also Jan., 1843, issue.

76. Hans Küng, *Infallible? An Inquiry* (Doubleday & Company, Inc., 1971).

77. See André Philip, "The Revolutionary Change in the Structure of European Political Life," in Z. K. Mathews (ed.), *Responsible Government in a Revolutionary Age* (Association Press, 1966), pp. 115–129.

78. John R. Seeley, "Remaking the Urban Scene: New Youth in an Old Environment," *Daedalus* (Journal of the American Academy of Arts and Sciences), Fall, 1968.

79. Gen. 49:24; Ps. 23:1; Ps. 80:1; Isa. 40:11; Isa. 44:28.

80. See Herbert Marcuse, *Eros and Civilization* (Vintage Books, Inc., 1955), pp. 96 ff.

81. *Ibid.*, p. 126.

82. For example, *A Handbook of Christian Theology*, ed. by Halverson and Cohen (London: Fontana, 1960), has no article on sexuality or man-woman relationships.

83. Norman Brown, *Life Against Death* (Modern Library, Inc., 1959), p. 3.

84. Sigmund Freud, *Collected Papers*. Quoted in Brown, *op. cit.*, p. 4.